ادكار الصباح والمساء

THE PROPHETIC INVOCATIONS

...Is it not through the remembrance
of God that ḥearts find tranquility?

—Qur'ān (13:28)

أذكار الصّباح والمساء

THE PROPHETIC INVOCATIONS

للحَبيب عَبد الله بن عَلويّ الحدّاد

Compiled by
IMĀM ʿABDALLĀH IBN ʿALAWĪ AL-ḤADDĀD

Translation, Transliteration, and Commentary by
MOSTAFA AL-BADAWI

With a Foreword by
HAMZA YUSUF

THE STARLATCH PRESS

THE STARLATCH PRESS™
PMB 126
80 Burr Ridge Parkway
Burr Ridge, IL 60521
USA
phone/fax: 312.896.7403
www.starlatch.com
info@starlatch.com

Printed in the United States of America

ISBN: 1-929694-10-5 (PAPERBACK)
1-929694-11-3 (HARDCOVER)

Design by Abd al-Lateef Whiteman

Special thanks to Abdal Hakim Murad, Kamal Uddin,
Aqeel Ali, Ibrahim Abusharif, Affan Arain, Tareq
Mahmud, Uthman Hutchinson, Ibrahim Osi-Efa,
Azhar M. Usman, and Anas Osman.

CONTENTS

TRANSLITERATION KEY

ء	ʾ [1]	ر	r	ف	f
ا	ā, a	ز	z	ق	q[12]
ب	b	س	s	ك	k
ت	t	ش	sh	ل	l
ث	th[2]	ص	ṣ[6]	م	m
ج	j	ض	ḍ[7]	ن	n
ح	ḥ[3]	ط	ṭ[8]	ه	h
خ	kh[4]	ظ	ẓ[9]	و	ū, u, w
د	d	ع	ʿ [10]	ي	ī, i, y
ذ	dh[5]	غ	gh[11]		

ﷺ—Mentioned after the Prophet Muḥammad's ﷺ name and translated as "may Allāh bless him and grant him peace."

رضي الله عنه—Mentioned after the name of a companion of the Propht ﷺ and translated as "may Allāh be pleased with him."

---

1. A slight catch in the breath. It is also used to indicate the running of two words into one, e.g. *bismi'Llāh.*
2. Should be pronounced like the *th* in *think.*
3. Tensely breathed *h* sound.
4. Pronounced like the *ch* in Scottish *loch.*
5. Should be pronounced like the *th* in *this.*
6. A heavy *s* pronounced far back in the mouth.
7. A heavy *d* pronounced far back in the mouth.
8. A heavy *t* pronounced far back in the mouth.
9. A heavy *z* pronounced far back in the mouth with the tongue touching the upper two front teeth.
10. Pronounced by narrowing the passage in the depth of the throat and then forcing breath through it.
11. Pronounced like a French *r.*
12. A guttural *q* sound.

FOREWORD

IN THE NAME of Allāh, the Merciful, the Beneficent. O Allāh, we are incapable of praising You; You are as You have praised Yourself. All praise belongs to You alone. We ask You by Your Beautiful Names to shower Your beloved Prophet with prayers and peace. May the blessings and peace of Allāh be upon our master Muḥammad, the unlettered Prophet, his family and wives, the mothers of the believers, and his descendants and companions. May Allāh's blessings and peace be upon all of them, as long as He is remembered by those who remember Him.

There is a well-known tradition related in Imām Mālik's *Muwaṭṭa'* that Jesus, the son of Mary, peace be upon them both, said, "Do not sit in a gathering without remembering Allāh, for if you do, your hearts will harden, and a hard heart is distant from Allāh." The hardening of the physical heart occurs from lack of physical exercise and from eating animal flesh with fat. Similarly, the spiritual heart is hardened by lack of spiritual exercise and eating the dead flesh of other humans (which is the metaphysical reality of the act of backbiting).

The spiritual exercise of the heart is called *dhikru'Llāh*, which simply means "remembering Allāh." The practice of remembrance is a practice of recollecting another world and another time. When

Odysseus came upon the island of the Lotus-Eaters, some of his crew took one bite of the Lotus flower and were overcome with lethargy. As humans from all eras are wont to do, his crew forgot from whence they had come and that their journey was a return home. But one day all lotus-eaters must leave their dreams and wake up. "Glory to God, who has woken us from our sleep. This is just as the Merciful promised, and the Prophets have been truthful in their words," say the sleepers of this world when they are finally and forcibly removed from the poppy field of pleasure and forgetfulness. The newly awoken come to the realization that they were in fact accountable for every God-given breath, but they have squandered their entire lives foolishly or, worse still, spent them in malevolent deeds.

Breath is a Divine gift, and the tongue is the plane upon which the breezes of the breath blow. To speak we need a tongue, lips, and breath. To remember God, we need a heart. We have been given all four and reminded by Allāh in every Book of revelation that the reason we are created is to worship Him. In fact, everything in existence is initially created in a state of worship. However, because of their free will, humans can forget the reason of their existence. "And if you forget, remember," says the Qur'ān.

It is through remembrance that equilibrium is established in the soul. "Is it not by the remembrance of Allāh that hearts are stilled?" the Qur'ān rhetorically asks. Stillness, or *sakīna* in Arabic, is a result of several phenomena. The first is that when remembering Allāh, one often feels His presence. While this can be true of remembrance of anyone, the presence of Allāh, as well as that of the Prophets and saints, brings a stillness of the heart without comparison.

Another cause of *sakīna* is the actual presence of angelic beings and the absence of the demonic, brought about by *dhikru'Llāh*. In our modern world, we tend to shy away from mentioning unseen beings such as angels and demons, but lack of belief in something does not necessitate its non-existence. Angels are real; they love the remembrance of Allāh and will actually seek out places where He is being remembered in order to join in. Though unseen, their presence is felt by the worshiper.

Furthermore, the actual words themselves that are invoked to remember Allāh bring stillness to the soul. Ancient languages produce an effect that more newly developed languages generally do not. For instance, when one hears Arabic, or sacerdotal Greek for that matter, one is struck by the power of the sounds even if the meanings are lost. This is certainly not true for most modern tongues. Arabic in particular has a special effect on the heart. For example, the simple yet most profound Islamic statement of creed, *Lā ilāha illa'Llāh*, is composed of only three Arabic letters: *alif*, *lām*, and *hā'*. From these three letters, the words for "no," "god," "except," and the Divine name, "Allāh," are derived.

These letters are pronounced simply by moving the tongue up and down, lightly touching the roof of the mouth. In ancient Chinese medicine, this action of the tongue was believed to unify all of the meridian channels in the body and engender good health. In addition, throughout the first few years of life, an infant will commonly place its tongue on the roof of its mouth and pull it back down.

While these are interesting facts, there is a more fundamental reason why remembrance of Allāh affects us in such a positive way. Simply stated, the entire body craves Divine remembrance more intensely than anything else. Every cell in the body is individually in a state of remembrance. When the heart and its translator, the tongue, join in, harmony occurs.

There is no doubt that meditation and prayer from traditions other than Islam also have an effect. Many people experience worldly benefits such as lower blood pressure, less stress, and better sleep. What Islamic spiritual practice offers additionally is a pure, unadulterated tradition. Its authenticity is guaranteed due to its direct connection to its original sources preserved by an unbroken chain of transmitters.

When I was a young student of the New Testament at a Jesuit high school, my teacher, a brilliant Jesuit priest, Father Daugherty said, "I can guarantee only two words in the entire New Testament were uttered by Jesus," upon him be peace, "and they are '*Abba*' and '*Amen!*'" However, the primary sources of Islam have been rigorously authenticated and are unlike those of other religions in this respect. Thus, we can be absolutely certain that the formulas found in this book were uttered by our beloved Prophet, may the peace and blessings of Allāh be upon him, and were passed on to us, his community, for protection and peace. We need these prayers for our sanity and for our protection from the evils of the world.

The compiler of this text is the great Imām, Shaykh ʿAbdallāh ibn ʿAlawī al-Ḥaddād, a direct descendant of the Prophet Muḥammad, peace be upon him, as well as the well-known and loved clan of Bā ʿAlawī of Hadramawt, Yemen. Our Prophet, peace be upon him, said, "Toward the end of time, take to the people of Shām (Greater Syria) and if not them, then the people of Yemen." Today, it is acknowledged that the last two great bastions of traditional Islam on the Peninsula of Arabia Felix are Yemen and Shām. While there are some great scholars left in the Indian Subcontinent and in the Western Lands of Islam, such as Chinqīṭ (Sub-Saharan Africa) and Mali, the majority of traditional scholars lie buried in the earth, and their books remain grossly neglected.

This text is small but powerful in that it draws its words from the pure *sunna* (words, deeds, and actions) of the Prophet Muḥammad, peace be upon him, who remembered Allāh in all of his states. The Qur'ān, in turn, praises those who remember Allāh: *Remember Me,*

I will remember you, (2:152) *Those who neither buying nor selling divert them from the remembrance of Allāh…Allāh shall reward them for the best of what they did, and increase them in reward from His bounty,* (24:37-38) and *The believers are those, who when Allāh is mentioned, their hearts tremble…they will have degrees with their Lord, and forgiveness and generous provision.* (8:2-4) There is not a page in the entire Qur'ān that does not have some reminder for us; indeed, the entire Qur'ān is a reminder.

This text is a *wird*, which is commonly translated as "litany." *Wird* literally means "a place of water," and this meaning is telling. A watering place is visited regularly, not out of mere fondness but out of necessity. The spiritual aspirant should approach his *wird* with the same intense thirst and regularity as he would his watering place. As water satisfies the body's physical demands, so too does the *wird* bring the soul to a state of contentment and, eventually, delight. The Qur'ān is itself a *wird*, a portion of which should be recited by Muslims daily.

This edition is distinguished by the fact that its translator, Dr. Mostafa al-Badawi, spent a large part of his adult life in the company and under the guidance of Shaykh Aḥmad Mashhūr al-Ḥaddād, who was a direct descendant of the compiler of this *wird* and also himself a master of the inner and outer sciences of Islam. While this is a general *wird* that can be used without the supervision of a spiritual physician, I personally had the blessing of taking this *wird* from Shaykh Aḥmad al-Ḥaddād, may Allāh be pleased with him, during his blessed life of scholarship and spiritual guidance. In one blessed gathering held by the Shaykh, may Allāh be pleased with him, he told me that now is the age of *hawsāt*. I did not know the meaning of this word and asked him what it meant. He replied, "Mental instability as a result of leaving the remembrance of Allāh."

This *wird* is a healing and prophetic medicine from a doctor of the hearts, Imām ʿAbdallāh al-Ḥaddād, who learned his craft from true scholars of knowledge and deeds, until he himself became a master. According to an authentic *ḥadīth*, "Scholars are the inheritors of the Prophets," and an inheritor, as any Islamic jurist knows, is able to use the inheritance according to his own discretion. Thus, the scholars of this Islamic community are the inheritors of the last of Allāh's Prophets, the paragon of His creation, our master Muḥammad, peace and blessings of Allāh be upon him. Imām al-Ḥaddād was such an inheritor and has presented this text, blessed by virtue of being composed entirely of Divine and Prophetic revelation, and arranged as none but a master physician could be trusted to arrange. What is left for us is only to take the medicine.

It is as the poet said: *We heal ourselves with Your remembrance, and should we forget we are in relapse.*

—HAMZA YUSUF

الورد اللّطيف

Al-Wird al-Laṭīf

I

INTRODUCTION

IMĀM ʿABDALLĀH AL-ḤADDĀD is a well known ʿAlawī scholar from Hadramawt. To say ʿAlawī is to say Ḥusaynī in lineage,[1] Ashʿarī in *ʿaqīda*,[2] Shāfiʿī in *fiqh*,[3] and Ghazālī in behaviour.[4] As with other illustrious ʿAlawīs, Allāh made him known despite his wish to remain in obscurity. Yet the Imām once said to some of his close disciples that what they saw as fame was in fact not so, for had he really wished for fame and requested it from Allāh, he would have easily eclipsed all other scholars and saints on the face of the earth.

Imām al-Haddād was born in Tarīm, Yemen, in 1044 AH and by the time he was about thirty years of age, had already acquired the reputation of being the foremost scholar and saint of his time.

His main litany was *al-Wird al-Kabīr*, which he recited twice daily, after *Fajr* and *Maghrib*. Also his were the *Rātib*, *Ḥizb al-Fatḥ* and *Ḥizb al-Naṣr*. *Ḥizb al-Fatḥ* is concerned with purifying the heart by getting rid of the rust covering it, then acquiring virtues and practicing them to the full, hence its name: The Litany of the Opening. *Ḥizb al-Naṣr*, The Litany of Victory, was designed for protection against outward and inward enemies.

Al-Wird al-Kabīr being rather lengthy, the Imām composed a shorter version. In this, as in his books and spiritual instruction, the Imām foresaw the time when people would have neither the time nor the will to do all that was required. *Al-Wird al-Laṭīf* was therefore made for us, in this 15th century *Hijra*. It is short, taking no more than fifteen minutes to complete once one has become familiar with it, and is to be recited after *Fajr* and *Maghrib*. If this is not possible, it is to be recited once before and once after midday, whenever time is available.

This present work is intended to help the English speaker familiarize himself with the meanings of the various Prophetic invocations of the *Rātib* and some of their merits and benefits, in a format geared toward recitation. The transliteration is meant to be the nearest possible rendering of the actual vocal recitation. A word like *Nabiyyan*, for instance, when it comes at the end of a sentence, is pronounced *Nabiyyā*, so this is how it has been transliterated.

The Arabic (including the Arabic transliteration) differs from other languages in its being the language of the Qu'rān, the language that Allāh chose to make worthy of conveying His revelation. Revelation is eternal knowledge of reality expressed in human language. Its vehicle requires exceptional precision, depth, subtlety and malleability to render it adequate for the purpose. Furthermore, the manner in which Allāh and, to a lesser extent, His Messenger ﷺ use the language is of an altogether different order from its other usages. A single verse of the Qur'ān will have many superimposed layers of meaning. It may be used for protection from various inward and outward perils, for curing certain illnesses, for increasing certain kinds of provision, for *baraka*, and for the recompense promised for the recitation of each of its letters.

Knowing this, Muslims all over the world have always recited both the Qur'ān and the Prophetic invocations in their original Arabic, even when unable to understand the language, to make sure that they lose none of the secrets and *baraka*, much of which are lost in translation.

However, prayer is not limited to specific times or occasions; it is a constant communion with Allāh. Whenever we leave our house or cross the street, we ask Allāh for protection. When hungry we ask Him to feed us and when worried to reassure us. This kind of spontaneous prayer should not be subject to constraints of language or even style. The companions of the Prophet ﷺ felt entirely free to address their petitions to Allāh in their own words, or in the case of a bedouin, in his local dialect, despite having memorized the Prophet's words and making frequent use of them.

As with all the litanies of Imām al-Haddād, *al-Wird al-Laṭīf* is made up of nothing but the prayers of the Prophet ﷺ and the formulas that he instructed his community to recite mornings and evenings. It is therefore strictly in conformity with the *sunna*, and once it is well-rehearsed and becomes regular practice, one can rest assured that he is following the Prophetic instructions as to which *adhkār* he should use to begin and end his day.

NOTES

[1] The ʿAlawī lineage is the most authentic of all *sharīfian* lineages. Each ʿAlawī knows precisely who his ancestors are, up to Imām Ḥusayn, the Prophet's grandson.

[2] Imām Abu'l-Ḥasan al-Ashʿarī formulated the creed of *Ahl al-Sunna wa'l-Jamāʿa*, and his formulation remains, together with Imām Abū Manṣūr al-Māturīdī's, that of the great majority of Muslims today.

[3] Soon after the arrival of their ancestor, Imām Aḥmad ibn ʿĪsā from Iraq to Hadramawt, the ʿAlawīs adopted the Shāfiʿī *madhhab* in all matters of jurisprudence. They emphasize greatly the importance of acquiring a solid foundation in *fiqh*, for both women and men.

[4] When the ʿAlawīs saw Imām al-Ghazālī's *Iḥyā' ʿUlūm al-Dīn*, *Revival of the Religious Sciences*, they realized that Imām al-Ghazālī had made a full exposition of everything they wished to teach. They therefore adopted the *Iḥyā'* as their main teaching book in matters of *taṣawwuf*, which, in their view, is the practice of *Sharīʿa* with the utmost sincerity and the purification of the heart from all its ailments.

II

ARABIC & TRANSLATION

بِسْمِ ٱللَّهِ ٱلرَّحْمَٰنِ ٱلرَّحِيمِ (1
قُلْ هُوَ ٱللَّهُ أَحَدٌ ﴿١﴾ ٱللَّهُ ٱلصَّمَدُ ﴿٢﴾ لَمْ يَلِدْ
وَلَمْ يُولَدْ ﴿٣﴾ وَلَمْ يَكُن لَّهُۥ كُفُوًا أَحَدٌ ﴿٤﴾ (ثلاثاً)

In the Name of Allāh, the Most Merciful, the Compassionate. Say: He, Allāh, is One. Allāh is the eternally Besought. He has not begotten, nor been begotten, and equal to Him there is none. (112)

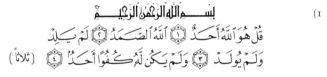

2) بِسْمِ ٱللَّهِ ٱلرَّحْمَٰنِ ٱلرَّحِيمِ
قُلْ أَعُوذُ بِرَبِّ ٱلْفَلَقِ ﴿١﴾ مِن شَرِّ مَا خَلَقَ ﴿٢﴾ وَمِن
شَرِّ غَاسِقٍ إِذَا وَقَبَ ﴿٣﴾ وَمِن شَرِّ ٱلنَّفَّٰثَٰتِ فِى
ٱلْعُقَدِ ﴿٤﴾ وَمِن شَرِّ حَاسِدٍ إِذَا حَسَدَ ﴿٥﴾ (ثلاثاً)

In the Name of Allāh, the Most Merciful, the Compassionate. Say: I take refuge with the Lord of the daybreak; from the evil of what He has created; from the evil of darkness when it gathers; from the evil of the women who blow on knots; and from the evil of an envier when he envies. (113)

3) بِسْمِ ٱللَّهِ ٱلرَّحْمَٰنِ ٱلرَّحِيمِ
قُلْ أَعُوذُ بِرَبِّ ٱلنَّاسِ ﴿١﴾ مَلِكِ ٱلنَّاسِ ﴿٢﴾ إِلَٰهِ
ٱلنَّاسِ ﴿٣﴾ مِن شَرِّ ٱلْوَسْوَاسِ ٱلْخَنَّاسِ ﴿٤﴾ ٱلَّذِى
يُوَسْوِسُ فِى صُدُورِ ٱلنَّاسِ ﴿٥﴾
مِنَ ٱلْجِنَّةِ وَٱلنَّاسِ ﴿٦﴾ (ثلاثاً)

In the Name of Allāh, the Most Merciful, the Compassionate. Say: I take refuge with the Lord of men; the King of men; the God of men; from the evil of the withdrawing whisperer; who whispers in the breasts of men; of jinn and men. (114)

4) وَقُل رَّبِّ أَعُوذُ بِكَ مِنْ هَمَزَٰتِ ٱلشَّيَٰطِينِ ﴿٩٧﴾ وَأَعُوذُ بِكَ
رَبِّ أَن يَحْضُرُونِ ﴿٩٨﴾ (ثلاثاً)

And say: My Lord! I seek Your protection against the insinuations of the devils and I seek your protection against their approaching me. (23:97-98)

5) أَفَحَسِبْتُمْ أَنَّمَا خَلَقْنَٰكُمْ عَبَثًا وَأَنَّكُمْ
إِلَيْنَا لَا تُرْجَعُونَ ﴿١١٥﴾ فَتَعَٰلَى ٱللَّهُ ٱلْمَلِكُ ٱلْحَقُّ لَآ إِلَٰهَ إِلَّا
هُوَ رَبُّ ٱلْعَرْشِ ٱلْكَرِيمِ ﴿١١٦﴾ وَمَن يَدْعُ مَعَ ٱللَّهِ إِلَٰهًا
ءَاخَرَ لَا بُرْهَٰنَ لَهُۥ بِهِۦ فَإِنَّمَا حِسَابُهُۥ عِندَ رَبِّهِۦٓ إِنَّهُۥ لَا يُفْلِحُ
ٱلْكَٰفِرُونَ ﴿١١٧﴾ وَقُل رَّبِّ ٱغْفِرْ وَٱرْحَمْ وَأَنتَ خَيْرُ ٱلرَّٰحِمِينَ ﴿١١٨﴾

What, did you think that We created you in vain, and that to Us you should not be returned? But Exalted is Allāh, the King, the Real, there is no god but He, the Lord of the Throne, the Generous. And whosoever calls upon another god with Allāh, of which he has no proof, his reckoning is with his Lord; the disbelievers never succeed. And say: My Lord! Forgive and have mercy, for You are the Most Merciful. (23:115-118)

6) فَسُبْحَٰنَ ٱللَّهِ حِينَ تُمْسُونَ
وَحِينَ تُصْبِحُونَ ﴿١٧﴾ وَلَهُ ٱلْحَمْدُ فِى ٱلسَّمَٰوَٰتِ وَٱلْأَرْضِ
وَعَشِيًّا وَحِينَ تُظْهِرُونَ ﴿١٨﴾ يُخْرِجُ ٱلْحَىَّ مِنَ ٱلْمَيِّتِ وَيُخْرِجُ
ٱلْمَيِّتَ مِنَ ٱلْحَىِّ وَيُحْىِ ٱلْأَرْضَ بَعْدَ مَوْتِهَا
وَكَذَٰلِكَ تُخْرَجُونَ ﴿١٩﴾

So glorify Allāh when evening comes upon you and when morning comes upon you. To Him belongs all praise in the heavens and the earth. [Glorify Him] in the evenings and high noon. He brings forth the living from the dead, and He brings forth the dead from the living, and He revives the earth after it is dead; even so you shall be brought forth. (30:17-19)

7) أَعُوذُ بِاللّٰهِ السَّمِيعِ العَلِيمِ مِنَ الشَّيطَانِ الرَّجِيم (ثلاثاً) *

I seek Allāh's protection, Who is the Hearer, the Knower, from the repudiate Devil.

(8 لَوْ أَنزَلْنَا هَٰذَا
ٱلْقُرْءَانَ عَلَىٰ جَبَلٍ لَّرَأَيْتَهُۥ خَٰشِعًا مُّتَصَدِّعًا مِّنْ خَشْيَةِ
ٱللَّهِ ۚ وَتِلْكَ ٱلْأَمْثَٰلُ نَضْرِبُهَا لِلنَّاسِ لَعَلَّهُمْ يَتَفَكَّرُونَ
﴿٢١﴾ هُوَ ٱللَّهُ ٱلَّذِى لَآ إِلَٰهَ إِلَّا هُوَ ۖ عَٰلِمُ ٱلْغَيْبِ وَٱلشَّهَٰدَةِ ۖ
هُوَ ٱلرَّحْمَٰنُ ٱلرَّحِيمُ ﴿٢٢﴾ هُوَ ٱللَّهُ ٱلَّذِى لَآ إِلَٰهَ إِلَّا هُوَ
ٱلْمَلِكُ ٱلْقُدُّوسُ ٱلسَّلَٰمُ ٱلْمُؤْمِنُ ٱلْمُهَيْمِنُ ٱلْعَزِيزُ
ٱلْجَبَّارُ ٱلْمُتَكَبِّرُ ۚ سُبْحَٰنَ ٱللَّهِ عَمَّا يُشْرِكُونَ
﴿٢٣﴾ هُوَ ٱللَّهُ ٱلْخَٰلِقُ ٱلْبَارِئُ ٱلْمُصَوِّرُ ۖ لَهُ ٱلْأَسْمَآءُ ٱلْحُسْنَىٰ ۚ
يُسَبِّحُ لَهُۥ مَا فِى ٱلسَّمَٰوَٰتِ وَٱلْأَرْضِ ۖ وَهُوَ ٱلْعَزِيزُ ٱلْحَكِيمُ ﴿٢٤﴾

Had We sent down this Qur'ān upon a mountain, you would have seen it humbled, split asunder out of the fear of Allāh. And those examples, We strike them for people that they may reflect. He is Allāh; there is no god but He. He is the Knower of the unseen and the visible; He is the All-Merciful the Compassionate. He is Allāh; there is no god but He. He is the King, the Holy, the Peace, the Faithful, the Sovereign, the Eminent, the Compeller, the Proud. Transcendent is Allāh beyond what they associate. He is Allāh, the Creator, the Fashioner, the Shaper. To Him belong the Most Beautiful Names. All that is in the heavens and the earth magnifies Him. He is the August, the Wise. (59:21-24)

9) سَلَٰمٌ عَلَىٰ نُوحٖ فِي ٱلۡعَٰلَمِينَ ﴿٧٩﴾ إِنَّا كَذَٰلِكَ نَجۡزِي ٱلۡمُحۡسِنِينَ ﴿٨٠﴾
إِنَّهُۥ مِنۡ عِبَادِنَا ٱلۡمُؤۡمِنِينَ ﴿٨١﴾

Peace be upon Noah among all beings. This is how We recompense those who excel, he was one of Our believing slaves. (37:79-81)

10) أَعُوذُ بِكَلِمَاتِ اللهِ التَّامَّاتِ مِن شَرِّ مَا خَلَق (ثلاثاً) *

I take refuge in the complete words of Allāh from the evil in what He has created.

11) بِسمِ اللهِ الَّذِي لا يَضُرُّ مَعَ اسْمِهِ شَيءٌ في الأَرضِ ولا في السَّمَاءِ، وَهُوَ السَّمِيعُ
العَلِيم (ثلاثاً) *

In the Name of Allāh, with Whose Name nothing on earth or in heaven can harm. He is the Hearer, the Knower.

12) اللّهُمَّ إنِّي أَصْبَحْتُ مِنْكَ في نِعْمَةٍ وَعَافِيَةٍ وَسِتْرٍ، فَأَتِمَّ نِعْمَتَكَ عَليَّ وَعافِيَتَكَ
وَسِتْرَكَ في الدُّنيا وَالآخِرَةِ (ثلاثاً) *

O Allāh! As Morning comes upon me I dwell in Your favour, well-being, and protection, so complete Your favour upon me, Your well-being and Your protection, in this world and the next!

13) اللّهُمَّ إنّي أَصْبَحْتُ أُشْهِدُكَ، وَأُشْهِدُ حَمَلَةَ عَرْشِكَ، وَملائِكَتَكَ، وَجَميعَ خَلقِكَ، أَنَّكَ أَنتَ الله، لا إله إلا أَنتَ، وَحْدَكَ لا شَريكَ لَكَ، وَأَنَّ مُحَمَّداً عَبدُكَ وَرَسُولُك (أربعاً) ✻

O Allāh! As morning comes upon me, I bear witness before You and before the Carriers of Your Throne, and Your angels, and all Your creation, that You are Allāh, that there is no god but You, Alone, with no partners, and that Muḥammad is Your slave and messenger.

14) الحَمْدُ لِلّهِ رَبِّ العَالَمِين، حَمْداً يُوافي نِعَمَهُ وَيُكَافِئُ مَزيدَه (ثلاثاً) ✻

Praise and thanks be to Allāh, Lord of the Worlds, with a praise that is adequate to His favours and equal to His increase.

15) آمَنتُ باللّهِ العَظِيم، وَكَفَرْتُ بِالجِبْتِ وَالطَّاغُوت، وَاسْتَمْسَكتُ بِالعُرْوَةِ الوُثقى، لا انفِصَامَ لَهَا، وَاللهُ سَمِيعٌ عَلِيم (ثلاثاً) ✻

I believe in Allāh the Formidable, and I denounce the idols and the sorcerers, and I hold fast to the firmest handhold, that which does not break, and Allāh is Hearer and Knower.

16) رَضِيتُ بِاللّهِ رَبّاً ، وَبِالإسلامِ دِيناً ، وَبِسَيِّدِنا مُحَمَّدٍ صَلَّى اللهُ عَلَيهِ وَسَلَّمَ، نَبِيّاً وَرَسُولا (ثلاثاً) ❋

I am content with Allāh as Lord, with Islām as religion, and with our master Muḥammad, may Allah's blessings and peace be upon him, as Prophet and Messenger.

17) حَسْبِيَ اللهُ لا إلهَ إلا هُوَ، عَلَيهِ تَوَكَّلْتُ، وَهُوَ رَبُّ العَرشِ العَظِيم (سبعاً) ❋

Allāh is my sufficiency; there is no god but He. On Him do I rely; He is the Formidable Lord of the Throne.

18) اللّهُمَّ صَلِّ على سَيِّدِنا مُحَمَّدٍ وَآلِهِ وَصَحْبِهِ وَسَلِّم (عَشراً) ❋

O Allāh! Bless our master Muḥammad, his Family and Companions, and give them peace.

19) اللّهُمَّ إنِّي أَسْأَلُكَ مِن فُجَاءَةِ الخَير ، وَأَعُوذُ بِكَ مِن فُجَاءَةِ الشَّرّ ❋

O Allāh! I ask You for sudden good and seek Your protection from sudden evil.

20) اللَّهُمَّ أَنتَ رَبِّي، لا إله إلا أَنت، خَلَقْتَني وَأَنَا عَبْدُك، وَأَنَا عَلى عَهْدِكَ وَوَعْدِكَ مَا اسْتَطَعْت، أَعُوذُ بِكَ مِن شَرِّ مَا صَنَعْت، أَبُوءُ لَكَ بِنِعْمَتِكَ عَلَيَّ وَأَبُوءُ بِذَنبِي، فَاغْفِرْلِي، فَإِنَّهُ لا يَغْفِرُ الذُّنُوبَ إلا أَنت ❋

O Allāh! You are my Lord, there is no god but You, You created me and I am Your slave, I uphold your pledge and promise as well as I can; I seek Your protection against the evil that I have done; I acknowledge Your favours upon me and I acknowledge my sin, so forgive me, for none forgives sin except You.

21) اللَّهُمَّ أَنتَ رَبِّي لا إله إلا أَنت، عَلَيكَ تَوَكَّلتُ، وَأَنتَ رَبُّ العَرشِ العَظِيم ❋

O Allāh! You are my Lord, there is no god but You, upon You do I rely, and You are the Lord of the Throne, the Formidable.

22) مَا شَاءَ اللهُ كَان، وَمَا لَمْ يَشَأْ لَمْ يَكُن، وَلا حَوْلَ وَلا قُوَّةَ إلا بِاللهِ العَلِيِّ العَظِيم ❋

What Allāh wishes happens, what He does not does not; there is neither power nor ability save by Allāh, the High, the Formidable.

23) أَعْلَمُ أَنَّ اللّٰهَ عَلى كُلِّ شَيءٍ قَدِير، وَأَنَّ اللّٰهَ قَدْ أَحَاطَ بِكُلِّ شَيءٍ عِلْما *

I know that Allāh has power over all things and that Allāh encompasses all things in His knowledge.

24) اللّٰهُمَّ إِنّي أَعُوذُ بِكَ مِن شَرِّ نَفْسِي وَمِن شَرِّ كُلِّ دَابَّةٍ أَنتَ آخِذٌ بِنَاصِيَتِهَا ، إِنَّ رَبِّي عَلى صِرَاطٍ مُسْتَقِيم *

O Allāh! I seek Your protection from the evil of my soul and the evil of every creature on earth You have taken by the forehead; my Lord is on a straight path.

25) يَاحَيُّ يَاقَيُّوم ، بِرَحْمَتِكَ أَسْتَغِيثُ ، وَمِن عَذَابِكَ أَسْتَجِير ، أَصْلِحْ لِي شَأْنِي كُلَّهُ ، وَلا تَكِلْنِي إِلى نَفْسِي وَلا إِلى أَحَدٍ مِن خَلْقِكَ طَرْفَةَ عَيْن *

O Living! O Sustainer! I call upon Your mercy for succour, and from Your chastisement I seek refuge! Make good all my affairs and do not entrust me to myself or any of Your creation for the blink of an eye.

26) اللّٰهُمَّ إنِّي أَعُوذُ بِكَ مِن الهَمِّ وَالحَزَن، وَأَعُوذُ بِكَ مِن العَجْزِ وَالكَسَل، وَأَعُوذُ بِكَ مِن الجُبْنِ وَالبُخْل، وَأَعُوذُ بِكَ مِن غَلَبَةِ الدَّيْنِ وَقَهْرِ الرِّجَال *

O Allāh! I seek Your protection from sorrow and grief, and I seek Your protection from incapacity and sloth, and I seek Your protection from cowardice and avarice, and I seek Your protection from the stress of debts and the tyranny of men.

27) اللّٰهُمَّ إنِّي أَسْأَلُكَ العَفْوَ وَالعَافِيَةَ وَالمُعَافَاةَ الدَّائِمَةَ في دِينِي وَدُنْيَايَ وَأَهْلِي وَمَالِي *

O Allāh! I ask of You pardon, well-being, and constant safety in my religion, wordly life, family, and possessions.

28) اللّٰهُمَّ اسْتُرْ عَوْرَاتي وَآمِنْ رَوْعَاتي *

O Allāh! Cover my shameful things and assuage my fears.

29) اللّٰهُمَّ احْفَظْنِي مِن بَيْنِ يَدَيَّ وَمِن خَلْفِي، وَعَنْ يَمِينِي وَعَنْ شِمَالِي وَمِنْ فَوْقِي، وَأَعُوذُ بِعَظَمَتِكَ أَنْ أُغْتَالَ مِن تَحتِي *

O Allāh! Protect me from [the evil that comes from] in front of me, from behind my back, my right, my left, and from above me and I take refuge in Your Greatness from unexpected harm from below me.

30) اللّٰهُمَّ أَنتَ خَلَقْتَنِي وَأَنتَ تَهْدِينِي، وَأَنتَ تُطعِمُنِي وَأَنتَ تَسْقِينِي، وَأَنتَ تُمِيتُنِي وَأَنتَ تُحْيِينِي *

O Allāh! You created me and You guide me, and You provide me with food and You provide me with drink, and You cause me to die and You give me life.

31) أَصْبَحْنَا عَلى فِطْرَةِ الإِسْلام، وَعَلى كَلِمَةِ الإِخْلاصِ، وَعَلى دِينِ نَبِيِّنَا مُحَمَّدٍ، صَلَّى اللهُ عَلَيهِ وَآلِهِ وَسَلَّم، وَعَلى مِلَّةِ أَبِينَا إِبْرَاهِيمَ، حَنِيفاً، مُسْلِماً، وَمَا كَانَ مِنَ المُشْرِكِين *

We have risen this morning on the original pattern of Islām, on the Word of Sincerity, on the religion of our Prophet Muḥammad, may Allāh bless him and his family and grant them peace, and on the confession of Ibrāhīm, who was upright, a Muslim, and not an idolator.

32) اللّٰهُمَّ بِكَ أَصْبَحْنَا ، وَبِكَ أَمْسَيْنَا ، وَبِكَ نَحْيَا ، وَبِكَ نَمُوتُ، وَإِلَيكَ النُّشُور ❋
(وَيقُولُ فِي المَسَاءِ : وَإِلَيكَ المَصِير)

O Allāh! You made us live this morning and You made us live this evening. You make us alive and You make us die, and to You is the arising. [In the evening: '... and to You is the final end.']

33) أَصْبَحْنَا وَأَصْبَحَ المُلْكُ لِلّه ، وَالحَمْدُ لِلّهِ رَبِّ العَالَمِين ❋ (وَيقُولُ فِي المَسَاءِ : أَمْسَيْنَا
وَأَمْسَى المُلْكُ)

Morning has risen upon us and sovereignty is all Allāh's, and all praises and thanks belong to Allāh, Lord of the Worlds. [In the evening: 'Evening has fallen upon us and sovereignty is all Allāh's....']

34) اللّٰهُمَّ إنِّي أَسْـأَلُكَ خَيرَ هذَا اليَومِ، فَتْحَهُ، وَنَصْرَهُ، وَنُورَهُ، وَبَرَكَتَهُ، وَهُدَاه *
(وَيقُولُ فِي المَسَاءِ: هذِهِ اللَّيلَةِ)

O Allāh! I ask You the good of this day, its openings, victories, lights, blessings, and right-guidance. [In the evening replace 'day' with 'night.']

35) اللّٰهُمَّ إنِّي أَسْـأَلُكَ خَيْرَ هذَا اليَومِ وَخَيْرَ مَا فِيه، وَأَعُوذُ بِكَ مِن شَرِّ هذَا اليَومِ وَشَرِّ
مَا فِيه * (وَيقُولُ فِي المَسَاءِ: هذِهِ اللَّيلَةِ)

O Allāh! I ask of You the good of this day and the best of what is in it, and I seek Your protection against the evil of this day and the worst of what is in it. [In the evening replace 'day' with 'night.']

36) اللّٰهُمَّ مَا أَصْبَحَ بِي مِن نِعْمَةٍ أَو بِأَحَدٍ مِن خَلْقِكَ فَمِنْكَ وَحْدَكَ لا شَرِيكَ لَكَ، فَلَكَ
الحَمْدُ وَلَكَ الشُّكْرُ عَلى ذلِك * (وَيَقُولُ فِي المَسَاءِ: اللّٰهُمَّ مَا أَمْسى)

O Allāh! Whatever favours I, or any of Your creatures, received this morning, they come only from You; You have no associates, so Yours are the praises and Yours are the thanks for them all. [In the evening replace 'this morning' with 'tonight.']

37) سُبْحَانَ اللهِ وَبِحَمْدِهِ (مائة مرَّة) ❋

Transcendent is Allāh and by His praises!

38) سُبْحَانَ اللهِ العَظِيمِ وَبِحَمْدِهِ (مائة مرَّة) ❋

Transcendent is Allāh the Formidable and by His praises!

39) سُبْحَانَ اللهِ، وَالحَمْدُ لِلّهِ، وَلا إلهَ إلا اللهُ، وَاللهُ أَكْبَر (مائة مرَّة) ❋

Transcendent is Allāh, all praise belongs to Allāh, there is no deity other than Allāh, Allāh is Greater.

40) وَيَزِيدُ صَبَاحاً: لا إلهَ إلا اللهُ وَحْدَهُ لا شَرِيكَ لَه، لَهُ المُلْكُ وَلَهُ الحَمْد، وَهُوَ عَلى كُلِّ شَيءٍ قَدِير (مائة مرَّة) ❋

And to be added in the morning: There is no god but Allāh alone, with no partners, His is sovereignty, His is all praise, and He is powerful over all things.

III

TRANSLITERATION

1. Bismi'Llāhi'r-Raḥmāni'r-Raḥīm. Qul huwa'Llāhu Aḥad, Allāhu'ṣ-Ṣamad, lam yalid, wa lam yūlad, wa lam yakun laHū kufuwan aḥad. [3 times]

2. Bismi'Llāhi'r-Raḥmāni'r-Raḥīm. Qul aʿūdhu bi-rabbi'l-falaq; min sharri mā khalaq; wa min sharri ghāsiqin idhā waqab; wa min sharri'n-naffāthāti fi'l-ʿuqad; wa min sharri ḥāsidin idhā ḥasad. [3 times]

3. Bismi'Llāhi'r-Raḥmāni'r-Raḥīm. Qul aʿūdhu bi-rabbi'n-nās; maliki'n-nās; ilāhi'n-nās; min sharri'l-waswāsi'l-khannās; alladhī yuwaswisu fī ṣudūri'n-nās; mina'l-jinnati wa'n-nās. [3 times]

4. Rabbi aʿūdhu bika min hamazāti'sh-shayāṭīna wa aʿūdhu bika rabbi an yaḥḍurūn. [3 times]

5. Afa-ḥasibtum annamā khalaqnākum ʿabathan wa annakum ilaynā lā turjaʿūn; fa-taʿāla'Llāhu'l-Maliku'l-Ḥaqqu lā ilāha illā huwa Rabbu'l-ʿArshi'l-karīm. Wa man yadʿu maʿa'Llāhi ilāhan ākhara lā burhāna lahu bihī fa'innamā ḥisābuhu ʿinda Rabbihi, innahu lā yufliḥu'l-kāfirūn. Wa qul Rabbi'ghfir wa'rḥam wa Anta khayru'r-Rāḥimīn.

6. Fa-subḥāna'Llāhi ḥīna tumsūna wa ḥīna tuṣbiḥūn; wa lahu'l-ḥamdu fi's-samāwāti wa'l-arḍi wa ʿashīyyan wa ḥīna tuẓhirūn; yukhriju'l-ḥayya mina'l-mayyiti, wa yukhriju'l-mayyita mina'l-ḥayy, wa yuḥyi'l-arḍa baʿda mawtihā, wa kadhālika tukhrajūn. [3 times]

7. Aʿūdhu bi'Llāhi's-Samīʿi'l-ʿAlīmi mina'sh-shayṭāni'r-rajīm. [3 times]

8. Law anzalnā hādha'l-Qur'āna ʿalā jabalin lara'aytahu khāshiʿan mutaṣaddiʿan min khashyati'Llāh; wa tilka'l-amthālu naḍribuhā li'n-nāsi laʿallahum yatafakkarūn. Huwa'Llāhu'lladhī lā ilāha illā Huwa, ʿĀlimu'l-ghaybi wa'sh-shahādati, Huwa'r-Raḥmānu'r-Raḥīm. Huwa'Llāhu'lladhī lā ilāha illā Huwa'l-Maliku'l-Quddūsu's-Salāmu'l-Mu'minu'l-Muhayminu'l-ʿAzīzu'l-Jabbāru'l-Mutakabbir; subḥāna'Llāhi ʿammā yushrikūn. Huwa 'Llāhu'l-Khāliqu 'l-Bāri'ul-Muṣawwir, laHu'l-Asmā'ul-ḥusnā, yusabbiḥu lahu mā fi's-samāwāti wa'l-arḍi, wa Huwa'l-ʿAzīzu 'l-Ḥakīm.

9. Salāmun ʿalā Nūḥin fi'l-ʿālamīn, innā kadhālika najzi'l-muḥsinīn, innahu min ʿibādina'l-mu'minīn.

10. Aʿūdhu bi kalimāti'Llāhi't-tāmmāti min sharri mā khalaq. [3 times]

11. Bismi'Llāhi'lladhī lā yaḍurru maʿasmihi shay'un fi'l-arḍi wa lā fi's-samā'i, wa huwa's-Samīʿu'l-ʿAlīm. [3 times]

12. Allāhumma innī aṣbaḥtu minka fī niʿmatin wa ʿāfiyatin wa sitr; fa'atimma niʿmataka ʿalayya wa ʿāfiyataka wa sitraka fi'd-dunyā wa'l-ākhira. [3 times]

13. Allāhumma innī aṣbaḥtu ushhiduka, wa ushhidu ḥamalata ʿarshika, wa malā'ikataka, wa jamīʿa khalqiqa, annaka anta'Llāhu, lā ilāha illā anta, waḥdaka lā sharīka laka, wa anna Muḥammadan ʿabduka wa rasūluk. [4 times]

14. Al-ḥamdu li'Llāhi Rabbi'l-ʿālamīn, ḥamdan yuwāfī niʿamahu wa yukāfi'u mazīdah. [3 times]

15. Āmantu bi'Llāhi'l-ʿAẓīm, wa kafartu bi'l-jibti wa'ṭ-ṭāghūt, wa'stamsaktu bi'l-ʿurwati'l-wuthqā, la'nfiṣāma lahā, wa'Llāhu Samīʿun, ʿAlīm. [3 times]

16. Raḍītu bi'Llāhi Rabban, wa bi'l-Islāmi dīnan, wa bi-sayyidinā Muḥammadin, ṣalla'Llāhu ʿalayhi wa sallama, nabīyyan wa rasūlā. [3 times]

17. Ḥasbiya'Llāhu lā ilāha illā Huwa, ʿalayhi tawakkaltu, wa Huwa Rabbu'l-ʿArshi'l-ʿAẓīm. [7 times]

18. Allāhumma ṣalli ʿalā sayyidinā Muḥammadin wa ālihi wa ṣaḥbihi wa sallim. [10 times]

19. Allāhumma innī as'aluka min fujā'ati'l-khayri, wa aʿūdhu bika min fujā'ati'sh-sharr.

20. Allāhumma anta Rabbī, lā ilāha illā ant, khalaqtanī wa anā ʿabduk, wa anā ʿalā ʿahdika wa waʿdika ma'staṭaʿt, aʿūdhu bika min sharri mā ṣanaʿt, abū'u laka bi-niʿmatika ʿalayya wa abū'u bi-dhanbī, fa'ghfir lī, fa'innahu lā yaghfiru'dh-dhunūba illā ant.

21. Allāhumma anta Rabbī, lā ilāha illā ant, ʿalayka tawakkaltu, wa anta Rabb'ul-ʿArshi'l-ʿAẓīm.

22. Mā shā'Allāhu kāna, wa mā lam yasha' lam yakun, wa lā ḥawla wa lā quwwata illā bi'Llāhi'l-ʿAliyyi'l-ʿAẓīm.

23. Aʿlamu anna'Llāha ʿalā kulli shay'in qadīr, wa anna'Llāha qad aḥāṭa bi kulli shay'in ʿilmā.

24. Allāhumma innī aʿūdhu bika min sharri nafsī wa min sharri kulli dābbatin anta ākhidhun bi-nāṣiyatihā, inna rabbī ʿalā ṣirāṭin mustaqīm.

25. Yā Ḥayyu yā Qayyūm! Bi-raḥmatika astaghīthu wa min ʿadhābika astajīr. Aṣliḥ lī sha'nī kullahu wa lā takilnī ilā nafsī wa lā ilā aḥadin min khalqika ṭarfata ʿayn.

26. Allāhumma innī aʿūdhu bika mina'l-hammi wa'l-ḥazan, wa aʿūdhu bika mina'l-ʿajzi wa'l-kasal, wa aʿūdhu bika mina'l-jubni wa'l-bukhl, wa aʿūdhu bika min ghalabati'd-dayni wa qahri'r-rijāl.

27. Allāhumma innī as'aluka'l-ʿafwa wa'l-ʿāfiyata wa'l-muʿāfāti'd-dā'imata fī dīnī wa dunyāya wa ahlī wa mālī.

28. Allāhumma'stur ʿawrātī wa āmin rawʿātī.

29. Allāhumma'ḥfaẓnī mim bayni yadayya wa min khalfī, wa ʿan yamīnī wa ʿan shimālī wa min fawqī, wa aʿūdhu bi ʿaẓamatika an ughtāla min taḥtī.

30. Allāhumma anta khalaqtanī wa anta tahdīnī, wa anta tuṭʿimunī wa anta tasqīnī, wa anta tumītunī wa anta tuḥyīnī.

31. Aṣbaḥnā ʿalā fiṭrati'l-Islāmi, wa ʿalā kalimati'l-ikhlāṣi, wa ʿalā dīni nabīyyinā Muḥammadin, ṣalla'Llāhu ʿalayhi wa ālihi wa sallam, wa ʿalā millati abīnā Ibrāhīma, ḥanīfan, Musliman, wa mā kāna mina'l-mushrikīn.

32. Allāhumma bika aṣbaḥnā, wa bika amsaynā, wa bika naḥyā, wa bika namūtu, wa ilayka'n-nushūr. [In the evening: wa ilayk'al-maṣīr.]

33. Aṣbaḥnā wa aṣbaḥa'l-mulku li'Llāhi wa'l-ḥamdu lil'Llāhi Rabbi'l-ʿālamīn. [In the evening: amsaynā wa amsa'l-mulku li'Llāhi...]

34. Allāhumma innī as'aluka khayra hādha'l-yawmi, fatḥahu, wa naṣrahu, wa nūrahu, wa barakatahu, wa hudāh. [In the evening: hādhihi'l-laylati, fatḥahā, wa naṣrahā, wa nūrahā, wa barakatahā, wa hudāhā.]

35. Allāhumma innī as'aluka khayra hādha'l-yawmi wa khayra mā fīh, wa aʿūdhu bika min sharri hādha'l-yawmi wa sharri mā fīh. [In the evening: hādhihi'l-laylati wa khayra mā fīhā, wa aʿūdhu bika min sharri hādhihi'l-laylati wa sharri mā fīhā.]

36. Allāhumma mā aṣbaḥa bī min niʿmatin aw bi aḥadin min khalqika faminka waḥdaka, lā sharīka laka, falaka'l-ḥamdu wa laka'sh-shukru ʿalā dhālik. [In the evening: Allāhumma mā amsā...]

37. Subḥāna'Llāhi wa bi-ḥamdihi. [100 times]

38. Subḥāna'Llāhi'l-ʿaẓīmi wa bi-ḥamdihi. [100 times]

39. Subḥāna'Llāhi, wa'l-ḥamdu li'Llāhi, wa lā ilāha illa'Llāhu, wa'Llāhu akbar. [100 times]

40. Lā ilāha illa'Llāhu waḥdahu lā sharīka lahu, lahu'l-mulku wa lahu'l-ḥamdu, wa huwa ʿalā kulli shay'in qadīr. [100 times, mornings only]

الرَّاتب الشَّهير

Al-Rātib al-Shahīr

IV

INTRODUCTION

OF ALL THE litanies of Imām al-Ḥaddād, the *Rātib* is the most famous. It has in fact acquired the title "*Al-Rātib al-Shahīr*," "The Famous Litany."

It came to the Imām by inspiration and was composed on the night of the twenty-seventh of Ramaḍān 1071 AH which was *Laylatu'l-Qadr*, the Night of Destiny. The stimulus for its composition was a request by a student of the Imām, a man named ʿĀmir, from the Banī Saʿd, who lived in a village near Shibām. His purpose was to have a litany that would be a protection for all who recited it and would contain specific items pertaining to the beliefs of *Ahl al-Sunna wa'l-Jamāʿa*, to counteract the effect of the Zaydī invasion of Hadramawt (the Zaydīs being Shīʿa but holding the Muʿtazilite belief that human beings create their own acts and that this is why they are held responsible for the evil they commit). The orthodox position, on the other hand, is that humans intend their actions, but can only carry them out through Divine Power and Will, the secret of predestination lying beyond rational understanding and to be apprehended by direct spiritual vision in the life-to-come.

This is why Imām al-Ḥaddād says in his *Rātib*: "In the Name of Allāh, all praise belongs to Allāh, both good and evil are by the will of Allāh." Which means that everything happens by Allāh, for which He alone is to be praised, since good and evil are necessary components of life in this world, both being ordained by the Divine Wisdom and Will.

The *Rātib* was first instituted in ʿĀmir's village by the Imām's permission, then at the Imām's mosque at al-Ḥāwī in 1072 AH. It was recited in congregation after the *ʿIshā'* prayer, its sunnas and invocations, except in Ramaḍān, when it was recited before *ʿIshā'* to make room for the *Tarawīḥ* prayers.

The Imām said that the *Rātib* protected the town where it was recited and helped people obtain from Allāh all their requests. When he went on Ḥajj he instituted it in both Mecca and Madīna, and it continued to be recited there every night, near Bāb al-Ṣafā in Mecca, and Bāb al-Raḥma in Madīna, for years afterwards.

Sayyid Aḥmad ibn Zayn al-Ḥabashī said that he who would recite it with presence, reverence, certitude, and a strong intention, continuing with *lā ilāha illa'Llāh* to reach one thousand times (instead of the usual fifty) would not fail to have something of the Unseen unveiled before him.

Ideally the *Rātib* should be recited twice, once after *Fajr* and again after *ʿIshā'*, but at least once after *ʿIshā'* is acceptable. Al-Ḥabīb Aḥmad Mashhūr al-Ḥaddād used to give special permission to recite the *Rātib* at other times as well as in times of need or stress.

Innumerable people in difficulty have recounted how recitation of the *Rātib* with specific intentions brought them prompt succour.

Imām Aḥmad, son of al-Ḥasan, son of ʿAbdallāh al-Ḥaddād, wrote a lengthy commentary on the *Rātib*, then bid his son, Imām ʿAlawī ibn Aḥmad, to expand on it. The latter's voluminous commentary was printed a few years ago in Singapore in Arabic. A *sayyid* of the Jamal al-Layl family also wrote a brief commentary, and the famous scholar,

ʿAbdallāh Bā-Sawdān, a lengthier one. Both belong to the thirteenth century *Hijra* and were printed in Egypt.

Unlike the other litanies of Imām al-Ḥaddād, which are meant for individual use, the *Rātib* is intended to be recited in a group. Each unit is repeated thrice unless otherwise noted.

V

ARABIC & TRANSLATION

بِسْمِ ٱللَّهِ ٱلرَّحْمَٰنِ ٱلرَّحِيمِ ﴿١﴾ (1
ٱلْحَمْدُ لِلَّهِ رَبِّ ٱلْعَٰلَمِينَ ﴿٢﴾ ٱلرَّحْمَٰنِ ٱلرَّحِيمِ ﴿٣﴾
مَٰلِكِ يَوْمِ ٱلدِّينِ ﴿٤﴾ إِيَّاكَ نَعْبُدُ وَإِيَّاكَ
نَسْتَعِينُ ﴿٥﴾ ٱهْدِنَا ٱلصِّرَٰطَ ٱلْمُسْتَقِيمَ ﴿٦﴾
صِرَٰطَ ٱلَّذِينَ أَنْعَمْتَ عَلَيْهِمْ غَيْرِ ٱلْمَغْضُوبِ
عَلَيْهِمْ وَلَا ٱلضَّآلِّينَ ﴿٧﴾

In the Name of Allāh, Most Merciful and Compassionate. All praise belongs to Allāh, Lord of the Worlds. The Most Merciful, the Compassionate. Master of the Day of Reckoning. You only do we worship and to You only do we turn for help. Guide us to the straight path, the path of those whom You have favoured, not of those against whom You are wrathful, nor those who are astray. (1)

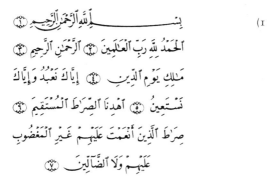

(2 ٱللَّهُ لَآ إِلَٰهَ إِلَّا هُوَ
ٱلْحَىُّ ٱلْقَيُّومُ لَا تَأْخُذُهُۥ سِنَةٌ وَلَا نَوْمٌ لَّهُۥ مَا فِى ٱلسَّمَٰوَٰتِ وَمَا
فِى ٱلْأَرْضِ مَن ذَا ٱلَّذِى يَشْفَعُ عِندَهُۥٓ إِلَّا بِإِذْنِهِۦ يَعْلَمُ مَا بَيْنَ
أَيْدِيهِمْ وَمَا خَلْفَهُمْ وَلَا يُحِيطُونَ بِشَىْءٍ مِّنْ عِلْمِهِۦٓ إِلَّا بِمَا
شَآءَ وَسِعَ كُرْسِيُّهُ ٱلسَّمَٰوَٰتِ وَٱلْأَرْضَ وَلَا يَـُٔودُهُۥ حِفْظُهُمَا
وَهُوَ ٱلْعَلِىُّ ٱلْعَظِيمُ ﴿٢٥٥﴾

Allāh, there is no god but He, the Living, the Sustainer; slumber overtakes Him not, nor sleep; to Him belongs everything that is in the heavens and the earth; who can intercede with Him save by His leave? He knows what is before them and what is behind them, and they comprehend nothing of His knowledge save such as He wills; His pedestal comprises the heavens and the earth, and it affects Him not to preserve them, He is the High, the Formidable. (2:255)

(3 ءَامَنَ ٱلرَّسُولُ بِمَآ أُنزِلَ
إِلَيْهِ مِن رَّبِّهِۦ وَٱلْمُؤْمِنُونَ ۚ كُلٌّ ءَامَنَ بِٱللَّهِ وَمَلَٰٓئِكَتِهِۦ وَكُتُبِهِۦ
وَرُسُلِهِۦ لَا نُفَرِّقُ بَيْنَ أَحَدٍ مِّن رُّسُلِهِۦ ۚ وَقَالُوا۟ سَمِعْنَا
وَأَطَعْنَا ۖ غُفْرَانَكَ رَبَّنَا وَإِلَيْكَ ٱلْمَصِيرُ ﴿٢٨٥﴾ لَا يُكَلِّفُ
ٱللَّهُ نَفْسًا إِلَّا وُسْعَهَا ۚ لَهَا مَا كَسَبَتْ وَعَلَيْهَا مَا ٱكْتَسَبَتْ ۗ
رَبَّنَا لَا تُؤَاخِذْنَآ إِن نَّسِينَآ أَوْ أَخْطَأْنَا ۚ رَبَّنَا وَلَا تَحْمِلْ
عَلَيْنَآ إِصْرًا كَمَا حَمَلْتَهُۥ عَلَى ٱلَّذِينَ مِن قَبْلِنَا ۚ رَبَّنَا وَلَا
تُحَمِّلْنَا مَا لَا طَاقَةَ لَنَا بِهِۦ ۖ وَٱعْفُ عَنَّا وَٱغْفِرْ لَنَا وَٱرْحَمْنَآ ۚ
أَنتَ مَوْلَىٰنَا فَٱنصُرْنَا عَلَى ٱلْقَوْمِ ٱلْكَٰفِرِينَ ﴿٢٨٦﴾

The Messenger believed in what was sent down to him from his Lord, and the believers; each one believed in Allāh, His Angels, His Books, and His Messengers, we make no division between any of His Messengers; and they said: We hear and obey, Your forgiveness O our Lord, to You is the becoming! Allāh charges no soul save to its capacity, to it what it has earned and against it what it has merited; our Lord, take us not to task if we forget or make mistakes; our Lord, charge us not with a burden such as You did lay upon those who were before us, our Lord, load not upon us that which we are unable to bear, and pardon us and forgive us and have mercy on us, You are our Patron, so help us against those who disbelieve. (2:285-286)

4) لا إلهَ إلا اللهُ وَحْدَهُ لا شَرِيكَ لَه ، لَهُ المُلْكُ وَلَهُ الحَمْد ، يُحْيِي وَيُمِيتُ وَهُوَ عَلى كُلِّ شَيءٍ قَدِير (ثلاثاً) ✻

There is no god save Allāh, Alone; He has no partners. His is sovereignty and to Him belongs all praise. He gives life and He gives death, and over all things He has power.

5) سُبْحَانَ اللهِ ، وَالحَمْدُ لِلهِ ، وَلا إلهَ إلا اللهُ ، وَاللهُ أَكْبَر (ثلاثاً) ✻

Transcendent is Allāh, all praise belongs to Allāh, there is no deity other than Allāh, Allāh is Greater.

6) سُبْحَانَ اللهِ وَبِحَمْدِهِ ، سُبْحَانَ اللهِ العَظِيم (ثلاثاً) ✻

Transcendent is Allāh and by His praises! Transcendent is Allāh the Formidable!

7) رَبَّنَا اغْفِرْ لَنَا وَتُبْ عَلَينَا ، إنَّكَ أَنتَ التَّوَّابُ الرَّحِيم (ثلاثاً) ✻

Our Lord forgive us and relent toward us, for You are the Ever-Relenting, the Compassionate.

8) اللّهُمَّ صَلِّ عَلى مُحَمَّد ، اللّهُمَّ صَلِّ عَلَيهِ وَسَلِّم (ثلاثاً) ✻

O Allāh, pray upon Muḥammad! O Allāh, pray upon him and give peace.

9) أَعُوذُ بِكَلِمَاتِ اللهِ التَّامَّاتِ مِن شَرِّ مَاخَلَق (ثلاثاً) *

I take refuge in the complete words of Allāh from the evil in what He has created.

10) بِسْمِ اللهِ الَّذِي لا يَضُرُّ مَعَ اسْمِهِ شَيءٌ في الأَرْضِ وَلا في السَّمَاءِ، وَهُوَ السَّمِيعُ العَلِيم (ثلاثاً) *

In the Name of Allāh, with Whose Name nothing on earth or in heaven can harm. He is the Hearer, the Knower.

11) رَضِينَا بِاللهِ رَبّاً، وَبالإِسْلام دِيناً، وَبِمُحَمَّدٍ نَبِيّا (ثلاثاً) *

We are content with Allāh as Lord, with Islam as religion, and with Muḥammad as Prophet.

12) بِسْمِ اللهِ، وَالحَمْدُ لِلّه، وَالخَيرُ وَالشَّرُّ بِمَشِيئَةِ الله (ثلاثاً) *

In the Name of Allāh, all praise belongs to Allāh, both good and evil are by the will of Allāh.

13) آمَنَّا بِاللهِ وَاليَوْمِ الآخِرْ، تُبْنَا إِلى اللهِ بَاطِناً وَظَاهِرْ (ثلاثاً) *

We believe in Allāh and the Last Day; we repent to Allāh inwardly and outwardly.

14) يَارَبَّنَا وَاعْفُ عَنَّا ، وَامْحُ الَّذِي كَانَ مِنَّا (ثلاثاً) *

Our Lord, pardon us and erase whatever we may have committed.

15) يَاذَا الجَلالِ وَالإِكْرَام، أَمِتْنَا عَلى دِينِ الإِسلام (سبعاً) *

O Possessor of Majesty and Generosity, make us die in the religion of Islam.

16) يَاقَوِيُّ يَامَتِين ، اِكْفِ شَرَّ الظَّالِمِين (ثلاثاً) *

O Mighty! O Invincible! Keep away from us the evil of the unjust.

17) أَصْلَحَ اللهُ أُمُورَ المُسْلِمِين ، صَرَفَ اللهُ شَرَّ المُؤْذِين (ثلاثاً) *

May Allāh remedy the affairs of the Muslims; may Allāh divert away from them the evil of evildoers.

18) يَاعَلِيُّ يَاكَبِير ، يَاعَلِيمُ يَاقَدِير ، يَاسَمِيعُ يَابَصِير ، يَالَطِيفُ يَاخَبِير (ثلاثاً) *

O You Who are High, O You Who are Immense! O You Who are Knowing, O You Who are Able! O You Who Hear, O You Who See! O You Who are Gentle, O You Who are Aware!

19) يَافَارِجَ الهَمّ، يَاكَاشِفَ الغَمّ، يَامَن لِعَبْدِهِ يَغْفِرُ وَيَرْحَم (ثلاثاً) ❋

O Reliever of grief! O Remover of distress! O You Who are to His slave Forgiving and Compassionate!

20) أَسْتَغْفِرُ اللهَ رَبَّ البَرَايَا، أَسْتَغْفِرُ اللهَ مِنَ الخَطَايَا (أربعاً) ❋

I ask Allāh for forgiveness, the Lord of all people, I ask Allāh for forgiveness of all wrongdoing.

22) لا إلهَ إلا اللهُ (خمسين مرّةً وإن بلّغها إلى ألفٍ كان حسَناً) ❋

There is no deity other than Allāh.

22) مُحَمَّدٌ رَسُولُ اللهِ، صَلَّى اللهُ عَلَيهِ وَآلِهِ وَسَلَّمَ، وَشَرَّفَ وَكَرَّمَ، وَمَجَّدَ وَعَظَّمَ، وَرَضِيَ اللهُ عَن أَهْلِ بَيْتِهِ الطَّيِّبِينَ الطَّاهِرِين، وَأَصْحَابِهِ الأَخْيارِ المُهْتَدِين، وَالتَّابِعِينَ لَهُمْ بِإِحْسَانٍ إلى يَومِ الدِّين ❋

Muḥammad is the Messenger of Allāh, may Allāh bless him and his family and grant them peace; may He honour, elevate, glorify, and magnify him. May He be well-pleased with his family, the good and pure, his Companions, the best of people, the rightly guided, and those who follow them with excellence till the Day of Reckoning.

(23 بِسْمِ ٱللَّهِ ٱلرَّحْمَٰنِ ٱلرَّحِيمِ

قُلْ هُوَ ٱللَّهُ أَحَدٌ ﴿١﴾ ٱللَّهُ ٱلصَّمَدُ ﴿٢﴾ لَمْ يَلِدْ

وَلَمْ يُولَدْ ﴿٣﴾ وَلَمْ يَكُن لَّهُۥ كُفُوًا أَحَدٌۢ ﴿٤﴾ (ثلاثاً)

In the Name of Allāh, the Most Merciful, the Compassionate. Say: He, Allāh, is One. Allāh is the eternally Besought. He has not begotten, nor been begotten, and equal to Him there is none. (112)

(24 بِسْمِ ٱللَّهِ ٱلرَّحْمَٰنِ ٱلرَّحِيمِ

قُلْ أَعُوذُ بِرَبِّ ٱلْفَلَقِ ﴿١﴾ مِن شَرِّ مَا خَلَقَ ﴿٢﴾ وَمِن

شَرِّ غَاسِقٍ إِذَا وَقَبَ ﴿٣﴾ وَمِن شَرِّ ٱلنَّفَّٰثَٰتِ فِى

ٱلْعُقَدِ ﴿٤﴾ وَمِن شَرِّ حَاسِدٍ إِذَا حَسَدَ ﴿٥﴾

In the Name of Allāh, the Most Merciful, the Compassionate. Say: I take refuge with the Lord of the daybreak; from the evil of what He has created; from the evil of darkness when it gathers; from the evil of the women who blow on knots; and from the evil of an envier when he envies. (113)

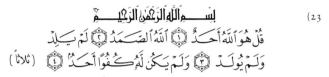

(25 بِسْمِ ٱللَّهِ ٱلرَّحْمَٰنِ ٱلرَّحِيمِ
قُلْ أَعُوذُ بِرَبِّ ٱلنَّاسِ ﴿١﴾ مَلِكِ ٱلنَّاسِ ﴿٢﴾ إِلَٰهِ
ٱلنَّاسِ ﴿٣﴾ مِن شَرِّ ٱلْوَسْوَاسِ ٱلْخَنَّاسِ ﴿٤﴾ ٱلَّذِى
يُوَسْوِسُ فِى صُدُورِ ٱلنَّاسِ ﴿٥﴾
مِنَ ٱلْجِنَّةِ وَٱلنَّاسِ ﴿٦﴾

In the Name of Allāh, the Most Merciful, the Compassionate. Say: I take refuge with the Lord of men; the King of men; the God of men; from the evil of the withdrawing whisperer; who whispers in the breasts of men; of jinn and men. (114)

(26 الفاتِحَةُ إلى كَافَّةِ عِبادِ اللهِ الصّالِحين، وَلِوالِدِينا، وَجَميعِ المؤْمِنِينَ وَالمُؤمِناتِ
وَالمُسْلِمِينَ وَالمُسْلِماتِ، أَنَّ اللهَ يَغْفِرُ لَهُم وَيَرحَمُهُم، وَيَنفَعُنا بِأَسْرارِهِم وَبَرَكاتِهِم . . .
وَإلى حَضْرَةِ النَّبِيِّ مُحَمَّدٍ صَلَّى اللهُ عَلَيهِ وَسَلَّم *

The Fātiḥa to all virtuous servants of Allāh, our two parents, all male and female believers and all male and female Muslims, that Allāh forgive them, have mercy on them, and give us benefit from their secrets and blessings.... [Then one makes as much duʿā' as one wants for oneself and all Muslims, then says:] And to the venerable Prophet Muḥammad ﷺ. [Once, then recite al-Fātiḥa once.]

27) اللّٰهُمَّ إِنَّا نَسْأَلُكَ رِضَاكَ وَالجَنَّة، وَنَعُوذُ بِكَ مِن سَخَطِكَ وَالنَّار ❋

O Allāh, we ask You for Your good pleasure and the Garden and we seek Your protection from Your displeasure and the Fire!

VI

TRANSLITERATION

1. Bismi'Llāhi'r-Raḥmāni'r-Raḥīm. Al-ḥamdu li'Llāhi Rabbi'l-ʿālamīn. Ar-Raḥmāni'r-Raḥīm. Māliki yawmi'd-dīn. Iyyāka naʿbudu wa iyyāka nastaʿīn. Ihdina'ṣ-ṣirāṭa'l-mustaqīm. Ṣirāṭa'lladhīna anʿamta ʿalayhim. Ghayri'l-maghḍūbi ʿalayhim wa la'ḍ-ḍāllīn. Āmīn! (1) [once]

2. Allāhu lā ilāha illā Huwa'l-Ḥayyu'l-Qayyūm; lā ta'khudhuhu sinatun wa lā nawm; lahu mā fi's-samāwāti wa mā fi'l-'arḍ; man dha'lladhī yashfaʿu ʿindahu illā bi'idhnih; yaʿlamu mā bayna aydīhim wa mā khalfahum wa lā yuḥīṭūna bi shay'in min ʿilmihi illā bimā shā'; wasiʿa kursiyyuhu's-samāwāti wa'l-'arḍa wa lā ya'ūduhu ḥifẓuhumā wa Huwa'l-ʿAlīyyu'l-ʿAẓīm. (2:255) [once]

3. Āmana'r-rasūlu bimā unzila ilayhi min rabbihi wa'l-mu'minūn; kullun āmana bi'Llāhi wa malā'ikatihi wa kutubihi wa rusulih, lā nufarriqu bayna aḥadin min rusulih; wa qālū samiʿnā wa aṭaʿnā, ghufrānaka rabbanā wa ilayka'l-maṣīr. Lā yukallifu'Llāhu nafsan illā wusʿahā, lahā mā kasabat wa ʿalayhā ma'ktasabat; rabbanā lā tu'ākhidhnā in nasīnā aw akhṭa'nā, rabbanā wa lā taḥmil ʿalaynā iṣran kamā ḥamaltahu ʿala'l-ladhīna min qablinā, rabbanā wa lā tuḥammilnā mā lā ṭāqata lanā bih, waʿfu ʿannā, wa'ghfir lanā, wa'rḥamnā, anta mawlānā fa'nṣurnā ʿalā'l-qawmi'l-kāfirīn. (2:285-286) [once]

4. Lā ilāha illa'Llāhu waḥdahu lā sharīka lah, lahu'l-mulku wa lahu'l-ḥamd, yuḥyī wa yumītu wa huwa ʿalā kulli shay'in qadīr.

5. Subḥān'Allāh, wa'l-ḥamdu li'Llāh, wa lā ilāha illa'Llāh, wa'Llāhu akbar.

6. Subḥān'Allāhi wa biḥamdihi, Subḥān'Allāhi'l-ʿAẓīm.

7. Rabbana'ghfir lanā wa tub ʿalaynā, innaka anta't-Tawwābu'r-Raḥīm.

8. Allāhumma ṣalli ʿalā Muḥammad, Allāhumma ṣalli ʿalayhi wa sallim.

9. Aʿūdhu bi kalimāti'Llāhi't-tāmmāti min sharri mā khalaq.

10. Bismi'Llāhi'lladhī lā yaḍurru maʿasmihi shay'un fi'l-arḍi wa lā fi's-samā', wa huwa's-Samīʿu'l-ʿAlīm.

11. Raḍīnā bi'Llāhi rabban, wa bi'l-Islāmi dīnan, wa bi Muḥammadin nabiyyā.

12. Bismi'Llāh, wa'l-ḥamdu li'Llāh, wa'l-khayru wa'sh-sharru bi mashī'ati'Llāh.

13. Āmannā bi'Llāhi wa'l-yawmi'l'ākhir, tubnā ila'Llāhi bāṭinan wa ẓāhir.

14. Yā Rabbanā waʿfu ʿannā, wa'mḥu'lladhī kāna minnā.

15. Ya Dha'l-Jalāli wal'Ikrām, amitnā ʿalā dīni'l-Islām. [7 times]

16. Yā Qawiyyu yā Matīn, ikfi sharra'ẓ-ẓālimīn.

17. Aṣlaḥa'Llāhu umūra'l-muslimīn, ṣarafa'Llāhu sharra'l mu'dhīn.

18. Yā ʿAlīyu ya Kabīr, yā ʿAlīmu ya Qadīr, yā Samīʿu yā Baṣīr, yā Laṭīfu yā Khabīr.

19. Yā Fārija'l-hamm! Yā Kāshifa'l-ghamm! Yā Man li'abdihi yaghfiru wa yarḥam!

20. Astaghfiru'Llāha Rabba'l-barāyā, astaghfiru'Llāha min al-khaṭāyā. [4 times]

21. Lā ilāha illa'Llāh. [50 or 1000 times]

22. Muḥammadun Rasūlu'Llāhi, ṣalla'Llāhu 'alayhi wa ālihi wa sallama, wa sharrafa wa karrama, wa majjada wa 'aẓẓama, wa raḍiya 'an ahli baytihi'ṭ-ṭayyibīna'ṭ-ṭāhirīn, wa aṣḥābihi'l-akhyāri'l-muhtadīn, wa't-tābi'īna lahum bi iḥsānin ilā yawmi'd-dīn. [once]

23. Bismi'Llāhi'r-Raḥmāni'r-Raḥīm. Qul huwa'Llāhu Aḥad, Allāhu'ṣ-Ṣamad, lam yalid, wa lam yūlad, wa lam yakun lahu kufuwan aḥad.

24. Bismi'Llāhi'r-Raḥmāni'r-Raḥīm. Qul a'ūdhu bi-rabbi'l-falaq; min sharri mā khalaq; wa min sharri ghāsiqin idhā waqab; wa min sharri'n-naffāthāti fi'l-'uqad; wa min sharri ḥāsidin idhā ḥasad.

25. Bismi'Llāhi'r-Raḥmāni'r-Raḥīm. Qul a'ūdhu bi-rabbi'n-nās; maliki'n-nās; ilāhi'n-nās; min sharri'l-waswāsi'l-khannās; alladhī yuwaswisu fī ṣudūri'n-nās; mina'l-jinnati wa'n-nās.

26. Al-Fātiḥa ilā kāffati 'ibādi'Llāhi'ṣ-ṣāliḥīn, wa lī-wālidīnā, wa jamī'i'l-mu'minīna wa'l-mu'mināti wa'l-muslimīna wa'l-muslimāti, anna'Llāha yaghfiru lahum wa yarḥamuhum, wa yanfa'unā bi asrārihim wa barakātihim... wa ilā ḥaḍrati'n-nabiyyi Muḥammadin ṣalla'Llāhu 'alayhi wa sallam.

27. Allāhumma innā nas'aluka riḍāka wa'l-janna, wa na'ūdhu bika min ṣakhaṭika wa'n-nār.

VII

COMMENTARY ON THE TEXT

1. Merits of *al-Fātiḥa*

The Companion, Abū Rāfiʿ ibn al-Muʿallā ﷺ said: "As I was praying in the mosque the Prophet called me and I did not answer him, but I went to him afterwards and explained that I had been praying, whereupon he asked me whether Allāh had not said: *Respond to Allāh and to the Messenger when he calls you*, (8:24) adding: 'Let me teach you the greatest *sūra* in the Qur'ān before you leave the mosque.' He then took me by the hand and, when we were about to go out, I reminded him of his saying that he would teach me the greatest *sūra* in the Qur'ān. He said: '*It is, Al-ḥamdu li'Llāhi Rabbi'l-ʿālamīn*, these are the seven oft-repeated verses (*al-sabʿ al-mathānī*) and the Formidable Qur'ān which was given to me.'"

Ibn ʿAbbās ﷺ recounted that once Gabriel, upon him be peace, was sitting with the Prophet ﷺ and heard a sound above him, at which he raised his head and said: "This is a gate opened in heaven today which has never been opened before." Then an angel descended through it and he continued: "This is an angel who has come down to earth, who has never come down before." The angel greeted them with *salām*, then said: "Rejoice in two lights given to you which were never given to any Prophet before you: *Fātiḥatu'l-Kitāb* and the last verses of *sūrat al-Baqara*. No portion of them will you ever recite without being accorded it."

Said Abū Hurayra ﵁: "I have heard the Messenger of Allāh ﷺ say: 'Allāh—Exalted is He!—says: "I have divided the prayer in two between Myself and My slave, and to My slave [I grant] what he asks.

"'"Half of it is Mine and half My slave's."

"'When the slave says: "*All Praise belongs to Allāh, Lord of all the Worlds*," Allāh says: "My slave praises [and thanks] Me!" When he says: "*The Most Merciful, the Compassionate*," He says: "My slave lauds Me!" When he says: "*Master of the Day of Reckoning*," He says: "My slave glorifies Me!" When he says: "*You only do we worship and to You only do we turn for help*," He says: "This one is between Me and My slave, and My slave shall be granted his request!" And when he says: "*Guide us to the straight path, the path of those whom You have favoured, not of those against whom You are wrathful, nor those who are astray*," He says: "This is for My slave and My slave shall be granted his request!"'"

And the Prophet ﷺ spoke to Ubayy ibn Kaʿb ﵁ thus: "By Him in Whose Hand my soul is, nothing like it was revealed in the Torah, Gospel, Psalms, or the Furqān. It is the seven oft-repeated verses and the Formidable Qur'ān which I have been given."

As for *āmīn*, it means, "Hear us and respond!" The Prophet ﷺ said: "When the Imām says: *āmīn* repeat after him, for he whose *āmīn* coincides with that of the angels, his sins are forgiven."

2. Merits of *Āyat al-Kursī*

Said the great Companion, Ubayy ibn Kaʿb ﵁: "The Messenger of Allāh ﷺ once asked: 'Abu'l-Mundhir, do you know which verse of the Book of Allāh that you have is the greatest?' I replied: 'Allāh and His

Messenger know best!' He repeated his question and I said: '*Allāh, there is no god but He, the Living, the Sustainer?*' Thereupon he struck me on the breast, saying: 'May knowledge be your delight, O Abu'l-Mundhir!'"

When asked which *sūra* of the Qur'ān was greatest, the Prophet ﷺ answered: "*Qul huwa'Llāhu Aḥad.*" Then when asked which verse of the Qur'ān was greatest, he answered: "*Allāhu lā ilāha illā Huwa'l-Ḥayyu'l-Qayyūm.*" The same man then asked which verse he should be given to bring good to him and his people and the reply was: "The end of *sūrat al-Baqara*, for it is one of the treasures of Allāh's mercy from under His Throne, which He gave to His people, and there is no good in this world or the next which it does not include."

3. Merits of the last two verses of *sūrat al-Baqara*

The Prophet ﷺ said: "Two thousand years before creating the heavens and the earth Allāh inscribed a book, two verses of which He sent down with which He concluded *sūrat al-Baqara*. The devil will not come near a house in which they are recited three nights."

And he said: "Allāh concludes *sūrat al-Baqara* with two verses which I have been given from His treasure which is under His Throne; so learn them and teach them to your womenfolk, for they are a blessing, a means to draw near and a prayer."

And he said: "If anyone recites the last two verses of *sūrat al-Baqara* at night they will avert harm from him."

4. Merits of the invocation

The Prophet ﷺ said: "He who says in the morning, *Lā ilāha illa'Llāhu waḥdahu lā sharīka lah, lahu'l-mulku wa lahu'l-ḥamd, yuḥyī wa yumītu wa huwa ʿalā kulli shay'in qadīr*, his will be the equivalent of freeing ten slaves of the Children of Ishmael, ten good deeds will be recorded for him, ten bad ones erased, he will be raised ten degrees, and he will be protected from the Devil until nightfall. Should he say it in the evening he will receive the same until morning."

5. Merits of the invocation

The Prophet ﷺ said: "To say *Subḥān'Allāh, wa'l-ḥamdu li'Llāh, wa lā ilāha illa'Llāh, wa'Llāhu akbar*, is more pleasing to me than everything else under the sun."

He also said: "The best of speech is *Subḥān'Allāh, wa'l-ḥamdu li'Llāh, wa lā ilāha illa'Llāh, wa'Llāhu akbar.*"

And he said: "I met Abraham on the night I was made to journey, and he said: 'O Muḥammad! Convey my greetings to your community and inform them that the Garden has pleasing soil and sweet water and that it is made of fertile meadows and planted with *Subḥān'Allāh, wa'l-ḥamdu li'Llāh, wa lā ilāha illa'Llāh, wa'Llāhu akbar.*'"

And he said: "In the Garden there are fertile meadows, so plant in them in abundance." They said: "O Messenger of Allāh, how shall we plant in them?" He replied: "With *Subḥān'Allāh, wa'l-ḥamdu li'Llāh, wa lā ilāha illa'Llāh, wa'Llāhu akbar.*"

And he said: "Allāh has selected four out of all words *Subḥān'Allāh, wa'l-ḥamdu li'Llāh, wa lā ilāha illa'Llāh, wa'Llāhu akbar*. He who says *Subḥān'Allāh!* twenty good deeds are written to his credit and twenty bad ones erased. To him who says, *Allāhu akbar!* the same also happens. To him who says, *lā ilāha illa'Llāh!* the same also happens. To him who says of his own accord, *al-ḥamdu li'Llāhi Rabbi'l-ʿālamīn!*, thirty good deeds are recorded and thirty bad ones erased."

6. Merits of the invocation

The Prophet ﷺ said: "Two words, light on the tongue, heavy in the scale, and dear to the All-Merciful: *Subḥān'Allāhi wa biḥamdihi, Subḥān'Allāhi'l-ʿAẓīm.*"

This is the last *ḥadīth* in Bukhārī's compilation. The meaning is: Transcendent is Allāh beyond our ability to praise Him; therefore, we praise Him by His praises of Himself, since none knows Him truly but Himself. Transcendent is Allāh, Formidable beyond conception, Great beyond words, utterly Incomparable.

7. Merits of the invocation

Allāh says in the Qur'ān: *Ask forgiveness of your Lord, then repent to Him....* (11:3) The order to ask for Allāh's forgiveness is very frequently followed by an order to repent. As Allāh says on the tongue of His Prophet Hūd (upon whom be peace): *O my people, ask forgiveness of your Lord, then repent to Him, and He will send upon you the skies pouring abundant rain, and He will increase you in strength unto your strength.* (11:52)

This is because when one asks for forgiveness and is granted it, and then commits the same errors or sins again, he becomes as one who makes a mockery of Divine orders and prohibitions, thus deserving severe chastisement. But when one follows his request for forgiveness by repentance, then conversely, he rises in the sight of Allāh and his evil deeds are converted in his book into good ones.

Repentance consists of regretting the wrong one has committed, repairing it if it be concerned with another person's right, and forming a strong intention never to fall into the same error again. Even if, because of human weakness, one falls into the same error again, one should repeat the sequence of asking for forgiveness followed by repentance.

When these are sincere, then even if one relapses a hundred times, Allāh will forgive him a hundred times.

When repeating this invocation we should intend those errors which we are aware of and those which we might have committed while unaware or have forgotten.

Then we say: *"Innaka anta't-Tawwābu'r-Raḥīm,"*—You are the Ever-Relenting, the Compassionate. We call upon Allāh by these Attributes that He may accept our repentance and make it sound and permanent, through His Attribute the Ever-Relenting, then grant us guidance and success in following the straight path, and paradise, through His Attribute, *al-Raḥīm*.

8. Merits of the prayer on the Prophet ﷺ

The Prophet ﷺ said: "Gabriel came to me and told me that my Lord says: 'Will it not please you, Muḥammad, that none of your people will invoke a blessing on you without My blessing him ten times and none of your people will give you a greeting without My greeting him ten times?'"

The Prophet ﷺ also said: "He who invokes blessings on me once, Allāh will bless him ten times, ten of his sins will be remitted, and he will be raised ten degrees."

And he said: "The one who will be nearest to me on the Day of Resurrection will be the one who invoked most blessings on me."

9. Merits of the invocation

The Prophet ﷺ said: "He who says three times at nightfall, *Aʿūdhu bi kalimāti'l-Llāhi't-tāmmāti min sharri mā khalaq*, no harmful thing shall affect him that night."

10. Merits of the invocation

The Prophet ﷺ said: "He who says: *Bismi'Llāhi'lladhī lā yaḍurru maʿasmihi shay'un fi'l-arḍi wa lā fi's-samā', wa huwa's-Samīʿu'l-ʿAlīm*, three times in the evening is safe from sudden afflictions till morning, and he who says it three times in the morning is safe from sudden afflictions till evening."

11. Merits of the invocation

The Prophet ﷺ said: "He who says every morning and evening, *Raḍīnā bi'Llāhi Rabban, wa bi'l-Islāmi dīnan, wa bi Muḥammadin nabiyyā*, certainly Allāh will satisfy him."

In Imām Aḥmad's *Musnad*, the same *ḥadīth* is quoted with the addition that it is to be said thrice in the evening and thrice in the morning.

And he said: "He who says in the morning, *Raḍīnā bi'Llāhi Rabban, wa bi'l-Islāmi dīnan, wa bi-Muḥammadin nabiyyā*—I shall be responsible for taking his hand until I lead him into the Garden."

12. Merits of the invocation

"In the Name of Allāh" means we know that everything in the universe happens by the Will of Allāh, in His Name, the Name of the King, and nothing can happen that He has not willed. With *Bismi'Llāh* everything begins.

"Praise belongs to Allāh" means that all that happens in the universe happens according to the infinite mercy, wisdom, and grace of Allāh. He is deserving of praise for everything in the universe whether, according to our perceptions, it is good or evil, for both are components of the total Divine plan, which is ultimately good, because it is willed by the Supreme Good.

This is the article of faith that contradicts the beliefs of deviant sects. It is why just as every act is initiated with *Bismi'Llāh* it is concluded with *al-ḥamdu li'l-Llāh*. Whatever begins by the Name of the Supreme Good must be concluded with thanks and praises to Him.

13. Merits of the invocation

This is a reaffirmation of two of the articles of faith, Allāh and the Last Day, following upon the affirmation of Divine Decrees in the previous invocation.

The implication of belief in Allāh and the Last Day is that we are ever-returning to Him, repenting to Him, and correcting both our inwards and outwards to conform to the pattern that will lead to security on the Last Day. Belief in Allāh means acknowledging that our upright behaviour comes from Him and that He remains there to receive us when we err and repent. Belief in the Last Day implies acknowledging that we must conform to the rulings of *Sharīʿa* to reach that day in a hopeful state.

14. Merits of the invocation

Yā Rabbanā: Calling upon our *Rabb*, Who is the Affectionate Protector, looking after His dependents, supervising them leniently, and rescuing them when they stumble.

Waʿfu ʿannā: Pardon us; do not punish us when we err. The difference between pardon and forgiveness is that to pardon is not to punish, while to forgive is not only not to punish, but also to conceal the error and protect from scandal. This is why the next request is: *wa'mḥu'lladhī kāna minnā*: Erase what we may have committed, erase it from our record and erase the evil consequences of it, whether inward in the heart, outward in the world, or later in the Hereafter.

15. Merits of the invocation

Divine Attributes are of two main kinds, Attributes of Majesty and Attributes of Beauty. Majesty is awesome, transcendent, implacable in justice and in exacting revenge, overpowering, and so on. Beauty is mercy, gentleness, forgiveness, grace, intimacy. Beyond both lies the ineffable Divine Essence.

To say: "*Yā Dha'l-Jalāli wa'l-Ikrām!*" is to call upon Allāh by both His Attributes of rigour and mercy. The Prophet ﷺ once heard a man saying: "*Yā Dha'l-Jalāli wa'l-Ikrām!*" He told him: "You have been answered; ask!"

In this prayer the Imām is asking for his life to be concluded in the right way when the time comes, that is to say, to die a Muslim. We are all enjoined to ask Allāh for a good conclusion to our lives (*ḥusn al-khātima*), since the most excellent life if concluded wrongly will be of no avail. The weakest moment in one's life is the moment of death and this is when one is most vulnerable to the action of the Devil. If one's faith is weak due to deviant beliefs, illusory attachments, sins, and so on, he may well succumb to the satanic onslaught of the last moment and die a *kāfir*. But he whose faith is strong, whose main attachment is to Allāh and His Prophet ﷺ, and whose behaviour is, in the main, in conformity with *Sharīʿa*, he will receive the support of the angels and men of Allāh and be able to resist the Devil's insidious attacks.

The Lord of Majesty is He Who has decreed death for all creatures, set a time for each, and causes them to die. None can give death but He. He is also the One Who created Satan. The Lord of Generosity is He Who grants His servants the graces of faith and good behaviour, Who casts into their hearts the love of Him, His Prophets and saints, and grants them firmness and support at the time of death. Yet they are both the same Lord, Allāh.

The meaning of the prayer is thus: "O You Who created men and the means for their salvation and perdition, Who made death ineluctable and followed by either perpetual bliss or torment, we acknowledge Your sovereignty, power, and justice, but we throw ourselves into the ocean of Your mercy, that You may save us from the evil ending and the Fire and grant us the good ending and the Garden." This is equivalent to the Prophetic prayer: "I seek protection in Your good pleasure from Your wrath!"

16. Merits of the invocation

"*Yā Qawī!*—O Strong!—O You Whose action in His creation is strong, Whose power is irresistible!"

"*Yā Matīn!*—O Invincible!—O You Who are invincible in Yourself, unaffected by any of Your creation!"

Both of these are Attributes of Majesty, and they are used to seek protection against the evil of the unjust, the iniquitous, and the tyrants, who are manifestations of other Attributes of Majesty; for He guides whom He will and He leads whom He will astray, He elevates some men above others and allows them to oppress them, He unleashes the tyrants to punish the people.

"*Ikfi sharra'z-ẓālimīn!*" *Ikfi* refers to His attribute, *al-Kāfī*, He Who suffices. In this context it is He Who suffices as protection against the evil of oppressors. Here again we are seeking the protection of a Divine Attribute of mercy against the manifestations of rigour.

17. Merits of the invocation

The Prophet ﷺ said: "No Muslim servant shall pray for his brother, unknown to him, without the responsible angel saying: 'And as much for you!'" And he said: "The prayer of a Muslim for his brother, unknown to him, is [always] answered. There is an angel standing near his head and whenever he prays for his brother a beneficent prayer the angel says: '*Āmīn*! And as much for you!'"

Whenever we make a prayer we should remember all the Muslim community, good ones and bad ones, Sunnī, Shīʿa, everyone. Whatever our differences, we are part of the organic whole that is the Muḥammadan Nation, and if the Prophet ﷺ cares for us, we should also care for each other.

18. Merits of the invocation

"*Al-ʿAlī*—The Most High," says Imām al-Ghazālī, "is the One above Whose rank there is no rank, and all ranks are inferior to Him."[1] He also says: "... Objects [are] divided into causes and effects, so that the cause is above the effect—above in rank; yet only the Cause of Causes is above absolutely."[2] This means that every cause is higher than its effect, which applies to chains of causes and effects. All causes in the universe are secondary causes; there is one First Cause with nothing above or before it, and that is Allāh. He is, therefore, High in absolute terms. Then Imām al-Ghazālī goes on to point out that Allāh uses examples from the material world to indicate higher realities and that when people are dim enough to take these literally, absurdities arise, such as assigning a spatial location to the Infinite. He gives an example of how one of those who take things literally would be discomfited if told that two distinguished individuals, one being superior in rank to the other, were sitting next to each other in an assembly. For: "... He might say 'this one sits above that one,' knowing that he only sits at his side. For he would only be seated above him if he were seated on his head...."[3] This is how one should understand how Allāh is "on" His Throne.

Al-Kabīr—The Immense. This is as much as to say the Infinite, for

He is Great in an absolute sense and nothing can be compared to His greatness. This is why it is said in a *ḥadīth* that the earth and terrestrial heaven are as a ring cast into the wilderness compared with the heaven above it. And the heaven above it is as a ring in the wilderness compared with the one above it. And so on, with every heaven until the Pedestal, within which the seven heavens and seven earths are as a ring in the wilderness. The Pedestal stands in the same relationship to the Throne. But the Throne, mighty beyond conception, stands as naught in the Divine presence. For it is finite and the finite is strictly naught before the Infinite. *Allāhu akbar*!

Al-ʿAlīm—The Omniscient—is He who knows everything, simultaneously, in the most minute detail and ultimate clarity. Any creature of His may know things only to the extent that He bestows upon it of His knowledge.

His knowledge does not arise from knowing things; rather, things arise as a consequence of His eternal knowledge of them.

Al-Qadīr—The Able—is He Who is capable of carrying out whatever He wills in exactly the way that He wills it. This attribute is usually mentioned in the Qur'ān as: *He Who has power over all things [or all acts]*.

Al-Samīʿ—The Hearer, or The All-Hearing—is He Who hears everything in the universe that is audible. He hears all sounds, those that are perceptible to human ears or to any other mode of hearing, simultaneously and distinctly, no sound impinging upon the other. He also hears the whisperings in the breasts and the prayers in the hearts.

The atom of hearing that He manifests in creation allows all creatures to hear what they hear, each according to the mode He allows them.

Al-Baṣīr—The All-Seeing—is He Who sees everything simultaneously and distinctly, what is visible to creatures and what is not. The atom of vision that He manifests in creation allows every creature endowed with vision to see, each according to the mode specific to it.

Al-Laṭīf—The Gentle, The Subtle, The Benevolent—is He Who executes His decrees in a gentle manner, wraps affliction in a cloak of mercy, attenuates punishments, relieves stresses, and grants ease within hardship.

Al-Khabīr—The Aware. He is the Knower Whose knowledge arises from knowing things from the inside; He knows the inward as part of omniscience, whereas *al-ʿAlīm* knows the outward aspect of things.

This invocation begins with praising Allāh with His attributes of transcendence, then His knowledge and ability, as if one were saying: "O You Who are beyond conception and beyond comparison, You Who are All-Knowing and All-Powerful, thus Able to do all things." Then we call upon His attributes of hearing and vision, as if to say: "You hear our pleas, You see our states!" Then we call upon His gentle responsiveness and awareness, as if to say: "Treat us with mercy, You Who are Aware of our feelings and innermost thoughts, give us what we want, remove our hardships, gladden our hearts!"

19 & 20. Merits of the invocation

The Prophet ﷺ said: "When a slave commits a sin, a spot is inscribed on his heart. Should he then refrain and ask forgiveness, it is removed. When he repeats it a larger one appears, until his heart is enveloped by it. This is '*That which covers,*' as Allāh the Exalted says: '*Nay! But that covered their hearts which they had earned.*'" (83:14)

The Prophet ﷺ said: "Hearts suffer from rust as the rust of copper; the polish of it is asking forgiveness."

And he said: "Iblīs said: 'By Your Might! I shall not cease to tempt Your servants as long as their spirits remain in their bodies!' He [Allāh] said: 'By My Might and Majesty! I shall not cease to forgive them as long as they ask Me for forgiveness!'"

Allāh says in a *ḥadīth Qudsī*, "... O My servants! You commit errors night and day. I it is Who forgive all sins; ask Me for forgiveness and I shall forgive you!"

21. Merits of *Lā ilāha illa'Llāh*

Ḥabīb Aḥmad Mashhur al-Ḥaddād, may Allāh be pleased with him, wrote in *Key to the Garden*, the book he devoted fully to an explanation and commentary on *lā ilāha illa'Llāh*:

Lā ilāha illa'Llāh. A phrase sublime in its meaning, brief in its construction, vast in its effect, noble in its rank, brilliant in its light, and unique in its merit. It comprises four words upon which the Faith is founded, and the *qibla* set. This is the phrase that was given in every Book sent down by God to every one of His noble Messengers, and through which one is rescued from the infernal Fires and wins eternal happiness in the Gardens. God the Exalted has said: *Know that there is no god but God!* (47:19) and *I am God, there is no god but Me, so worship Me!* (20:14) *God, there is no god but He, the Living, the Sustainer,* (2:255) *God, there is no god but He, to Him belong the Most Beautiful Names,* (20:8) and *We sent no Messenger before you without revealing to him: 'there is no god but Me, so worship Me'.* (21:25)

Through sound belief and certainty in its meaning, and by submission to it, one attains to faith [*imān*]. By uttering it with sincerity, and truly acting in accordance with it, Islam results. By attaining both sound belief and submission to its authority there dawns upon the heart the reality of *iḥsān*.

The phrase of *Tawḥīd* is also called the "Phrase of the Testimony," and of "Sincerity," "Reality," "Truth," "the Pledge," "Faith," "Piety," the "Good Word," the "Abiding Word," "God's Most Exalted Word," the "Word of Intercession," the "Price of the Garden," and the "Key to the Garden."

It is what a man enters Islam with first, and the last thing he leaves the world with, to the Garden and eternal bliss. As the *ḥadīth* says: "Whoever has for his last words in this life *lā ilāha illa'Llāh*, shall enter the Garden." It is the first obligation, and also the last. Whoever says it with certainty, and dies while persisting in it shall have the joy of entering the Garden, as this *ḥadīth* states. But whoever rejects it with arrogance, either by denial or polytheism, shall enter the Fire, and there is no worse abode.

Those who arrogantly refrain from worshipping Me shall enter Hell subjugated, (40:60) *As for those who were scornful and arrogant, He will give them a painful torment, and they shall find no protecting friend or helper against God,* (4:173) *God has forbidden the Garden to the one who ascribes partners to God, and his abode is the Fire.* (5:72)

Lā ilāha illa'Llāh means that God alone is worthy of worship. "God" [Allāh] is the noun which denotes the Holiest Essence, the Necessary Existent, Who is possessed of all the attributes of perfection and majesty, is free from all attributes of coming into being, of having partners, peers or likenesses, and from every attribute and state which does not befit His Glory and Magnitude. For He is the Unique, Eternal God, Who neither begets nor is begotten, Who has no likeness. There is no god but Him, praised is He beyond comparison; He has no partners in His Essence, Attributes, or Actions, to Him belong Sovereignty and all praise, Who has power over all things.[4]

He also writes in the chapter entitled: "The Effects of *Tawḥīd* and of its Noble Phrase":

The Two Testimonies are powerfully effective in refining the self, creating rectitude of character, and reinforcing social ties. The Testimony of *Lā ilāha illa'Llāh* liberates the mind from illusions, and purifies souls from the dirt of polytheism, so that they rise up from the mire of their devotion to other than God (Exalted is He!), and from the debasement which inheres in worshipping idols, animals, and men. Hearts are united by it in the adoration of one God, and faces are united in facing the same *qibla*. *Tawḥīd* thus has a beneficial effect in uniting the hearts of the human race and making them work together for the common good, and for the success of all. The Testimony of *Muḥammadun rasūlu'Llāh* and belief in his Message and in his Upright Book strengthen morality, reform souls, and set an excellent example to be followed in all situations.

These two utterances are the believer's treasure and capital, and are the source of his happiness in this life and in the next, for those who attain to the Truth in accordance with them, and draw light from their radiance in that which relates to *Tawḥīd* and achieving an attachment to the Holiest Presence [*al-Janāb al-Aqdas*] and to the advent of His spiritual gifts [*wāridāt imdādātih*], and set themselves in the way of the breaths of Union with Him and of His gifts of nearness. Similarly, through them there arise the consequences of following the Noblest Messenger, the Firmest Handhold [*al-ʿUrwat al-Wuthqā*], the Excellent Example, in every religious and worldly transaction, and in that which relates to what is good for one's daily life and one's abode in the Afterlife, whether this relates to the heart or the body, the individual or the community. Around the pivot of these Two Testimonies revolves the well-being of the human race in both abodes.

Know that this noble phrase has two halves. Firstly, there is a negation—*Lā ilāha* (there is no deity), and secondly there is an affirmation—*illa'Llāh* (except God). When the negation is enounced, followed by the affirmation, this signifies that a Muslim has acknowledged and established *Tawḥīd* in his heart by means of this noble phrase, which is incompatible with, and negates, the 'Greater Polytheism' [*al-shirk al-akbar*], the presence of which invalidates the foundations of faith. Faith is strengthened by repeating it with the heart and the tongue. The Prophet ﷺ said, "Renew your faith with *Lā ilāha illa'Llāh*!" It is also incompatible with, and negates, the 'Lesser Polytheism,' namely ostentation in worship, the desire to gain eminence and power over other people, and all other actions in which one pays attention to the regard of others, and desires their praise and respect, and hopes for status in their eyes. The Prophet ﷺ said that "Polytheism in my nation is more imperceptible than the footfalls of ants." This Lesser Polytheism does not invalidate the foundations of faith, upon which one's salvation depends, but simply renders it defective. *Lā ilāha illa'Llāh* destroys both the Greater and Lesser Polytheism in whoever utters it with sincere faith and acts accordingly. The fact that *Lā ilāha* comes first means that the heart is voided of these concealed things and these impurities. The subsequent affirmation of *illa'Llāh* adorns and fills up the heart with the lights of *Tawḥīd* and faith. It is therefore not surprising that holding fast to and repeating *dhikr* brings about the purification of the heart, its cleansing from blemishes, and its illumination. Good deeds are reckoned in accordance with the number of repetitions of the *dhikr*, each *Lā ilāha illa'Llāh* being counted as one, while their reward is ten times as much, or multiplied many more times. If a person engaged in *dhikr* bears in mind that *Lā ilāha illa'Llāh* is also a verse of the Qur'ān and makes the intention to recite from the Qur'ān together with doing *dhikr*, he gains the reward for Qur'ānic recitation also.

A subtle indication [*ishāra*] lies in the fact that the letters of the Testimony all arise from the depths of the body, and none of them are formed by the lips, which points to the fact that these should proceed from the purest inward part, the heart, not the lips. Similarly, none of the letters have dots, and this is an allusion to freedom from worshipping other than God.

Lā ilāha illa'Llāh; Muḥammadun rasūlu'Llāh consists of seven words. A man has seven members, and the Fire has seven doors, and each of the seven words closes one of the seven doors against one of the members.[5]

And Imām ʿAbdallāh al-Ḥaddād, may God be pleased with him, writes in *Gifts for the Seeker* under: "*Lā ilāha illa'Llāh* as a formula for *dhikr*":

You should know that this phrase is the most comprehensive and profitable of all invocations; the nearest to bringing about the Opening and Illumining of the heart with the light of God. It is also the most suitable of invocations for all people, since it includes the meanings of all other invocations, such as *al-ḥamdu li'Llāh*, *Subḥān Allāh*, and so on. Each believer should, therefore, make it his inseparable *wird*, his constant *dhikr*, without, however, abandoning the other invocations, of each of which he should have a *wird*.

Every human being is either a traveller, an arriver, or a non-traveller, and all three should hold unceasingly to this invocation. Travellers and non-travellers, since they perceive objects and attribute to them an existence of their own—something which may lead to subtle forms of hidden *shirk*—can only expel these from their souls by constantly repeating this phrase. As for the man who has arrived, this invocation is again the most appropriate for him, because although he perceives things by God, and unceasingly summons them to Him, he is not entirely free from perceiving his own self from time to time, and from reprehensible thoughts unworthy of his rank. It has been handed down to us that Abū Bakr al-Ṣiddīq رضي الله عنه used to insert this phrase into his conversation: he would utter a few words, say *Lā ilāha illa'Llāh*, and then resume what he was saying. This pertains to the Station of Subsistence [*baqā'*] which follows that of Extinction [*fanā'*]. As we said earlier, there is no invocation more appropriate for a man constantly to use than this; however, when the traveller reaches the initial stages of extinction, and is liberated from perceiving any of the worlds [as autonomous], then the most appropriate thing for him at that time is to keep to the Name of Allāh. This is what the people of gnosis have advised.

All the above is from the point of view of choosing the best and most appropriate alternative, for otherwise all the invocations are paths leading to God. The shaykhs (may God be pleased with them) have many methods of uttering this honourable Phrase, whether aloud or silently, and have set conditions which the invoker who would expose himself to the Divine effulgence and the Lordly Opening needs to fulfil. These are explained in those of their treatises which deal with them specifically, where they can be found by whoever wishes to tread the path of such men. It is best that those who are able to find in their time a shaykh of authority should receive these from him directly, since books are a last resort for those who are unable to find [such a teacher]; and what a difference there is between a man who receives the Path from a gnostic of authority who will take him to God, and one who only picks it up from a book!

God guides to what is right. To Him is the return, and success is from Him and in His Hand.[6]

22. Merits of the invocation

The completion of the testimony of faith, *Lā ilāha illa'Llāh*, is *Muḥammadun rasūlu'Llāh*, Muḥammad is the Messenger of Allāh. He said ﷺ: "He who testifies that there is no god but Allāh and that Muḥammad is the Messenger of Allāh—Allāh forbids the Fire to him." The completion of the second testimony is *ṣalla'Llāhu ʿalayhi wa sallam*, may Allāh send down His benedictions upon Him and His peace. These prayers are embellished by two more things; further prayers to honour, ennoble, glorify and magnify him, and also the inclusion of his household (that is his wives, children, and all his descendants), his Companions, and all those who follow them with excellence till the Last Day.

23. Merits of *sūrat al-Ikhlāṣ*

The Prophet ﷺ stated on more than one occasion that *sūrat al-Ikhlāṣ* was worth one third of the Qur'ān.

One of the Companions, leading an expedition, always ended his Qur'ānic recitations during the ritual prayers with *Qul Huwa'Llāhu Aḥad*. This was mentioned to the Prophet ﷺ on their return and he bid them ask him why he acted thus. He replied: "Because it is the attribute of the All-Merciful and I love to recite it." On hearing this the Prophet ﷺ said: "Tell him that Allāh loves him."

And on hearing a man recite, *Qul Huwa'Llāhu Aḥad*, the Prophet ﷺ stated: "It has become incumbent!" Abū Hurayra ؓ asked the Prophet ﷺ what had become incumbent and the Prophet replied that it was the Garden.

24 & 25. Merits of the *Muʿawwidhatayn*

The Prophet ﷺ said: "What wondrous verses have been revealed tonight! The like of them has never been seen. They are: *Qul aʿūdhu bi-rabbi'l-falaq* and *Qul aʿūdhu bi-rabbi'n-nās*."

ʿĀ'isha, may Allāh be pleased with her, said that every night when the Prophet ﷺ went to his bed he joined his hands and breathed into them, reciting *Qul Huwa'Llāhu Aḥad, Qul aʿūdhu bi-rabbi'l-falaq*, and *Qul aʿūdhu bi-rabbi'n-nās*. Then he would wipe as much of his body as he could with his hands, beginning with his head, his face and the front of his body, doing that three times.

Once as the Prophet ﷺ and some of his companions, may Allāh be pleased with them, were travelling in the desert, not far from al-Abwā' where the Prophet's mother is buried, they were enveloped by wind and intense darkness. Whereupon the Prophet ﷺ began to recite *Qul aʿūdhu bi-rabbi'l-falaq* and *Qul aʿūdhu bi-rabbi'n-nās*. He then turned to ʿUqba ibn ʿĀmir 🙶, who was with him, and said: "Use them ʿUqba when seeking refuge in Allāh, for there is nothing comparable to them to be used for that."

Another Companion recounted how they went out on a dark, rainy night looking for the Prophet 🙶. When they caught up with him he told him: "Say!" The Companion asked him what he was to say. He replied: "Say *Qul Huwa'Llāhu Aḥad* and the *Muʿawwidhatayn* three times morning and evening; they will serve you for every purpose."

To clarify the meanings of some of the expressions: the "women who blow on knots" are the sorceresses, and the "envier" is he who gives the "evil eye," both being kinds of injurious behaviour mediated by the subtle world. The "withdrawing whisperer" is the Devil. The *ḥadīth* states: "The Devil's trunk rests on the Son of Adam's heart. When he remembers Allāh, the Devil withdraws; when the Son of Adam forgets, he gobbles his heart."

26 & 27. Merits of the invocation

The Prophet 🙶 said: "When someone asks Allāh for the Garden three times, the Garden says: 'O Allāh! Make him enter the Garden;' and when someone asks protection from the Fire three times, the Fire says: 'O Allāh! Protect him from the Fire!'"

NOTES

[1] Imām al-Ghazālī, *The Ninety-Nine Beautiful Names of God*, trans. David B. Burrell and Nazih Daher (Cambridge: Islamic Texts Society, 1992), 102.

[2] Ibid., 104.

[3] Ibid., 105.

[4] *Ḥabīb* Aḥmad Mashhūr al-Ḥaddād, *Key to the Garden*, trans. Mostafa al-Badawi (London: The Quilliam Press, 1990), 3-4.

[5] Ibid., 26-28.

[6] Imām ʿAbdallāh al-Ḥaddād, *Gifts for the Seeker*, trans. Mostafa al-Badawi (London: The Quilliam Press, 1992), 18-19.

ARABIC APPENDIX I: *Al-Wird al-Laṭīf*

الورد اللّطيف

بِسْمِ ٱللَّهِ ٱلرَّحْمَٰنِ ٱلرَّحِيمِ

قُلْ هُوَ ٱللَّهُ أَحَدٌ ﴿١﴾ ٱللَّهُ ٱلصَّمَدُ ﴿٢﴾ لَمْ يَلِدْ
وَلَمْ يُولَدْ ﴿٣﴾ وَلَمْ يَكُن لَّهُۥ كُفُوًا أَحَدٌۢ ﴿٤﴾ (ثلاثاً)

بِسْمِ ٱللَّهِ ٱلرَّحْمَٰنِ ٱلرَّحِيمِ

قُلْ أَعُوذُ بِرَبِّ ٱلْفَلَقِ ﴿١﴾ مِن شَرِّ مَا خَلَقَ ﴿٢﴾ وَمِن
شَرِّ غَاسِقٍ إِذَا وَقَبَ ﴿٣﴾ وَمِن شَرِّ ٱلنَّفَّٰثَٰتِ فِى
ٱلْعُقَدِ ﴿٤﴾ وَمِن شَرِّ حَاسِدٍ إِذَا حَسَدَ ﴿٥﴾ (ثلاثاً)

بِسْمِ ٱللَّهِ ٱلرَّحْمَٰنِ ٱلرَّحِيمِ

قُلْ أَعُوذُ بِرَبِّ ٱلنَّاسِ ﴿١﴾ مَلِكِ ٱلنَّاسِ ﴿٢﴾ إِلَٰهِ
ٱلنَّاسِ ﴿٣﴾ مِن شَرِّ ٱلْوَسْوَاسِ ٱلْخَنَّاسِ ﴿٤﴾ ٱلَّذِى
يُوَسْوِسُ فِى صُدُورِ ٱلنَّاسِ ﴿٥﴾
مِنَ ٱلْجِنَّةِ وَٱلنَّاسِ ﴿٦﴾ (ثلاثاً)

وَقُل رَّبِّ أَعُوذُ بِكَ مِنْ هَمَزَٰتِ ٱلشَّيَٰطِينِ ﴿٩٧﴾ وَأَعُوذُ بِكَ
رَبِّ أَن يَحْضُرُونِ ﴿٩٨﴾ (ثلاثاً)

أَفَحَسِبْتُمْ أَنَّمَا خَلَقْنَٰكُمْ عَبَثًا وَأَنَّكُمْ
إِلَيْنَا لَا تُرْجَعُونَ ﴿١١٥﴾ فَتَعَٰلَى ٱللَّهُ ٱلْمَلِكُ ٱلْحَقُّ ۖ لَآ إِلَٰهَ إِلَّا
هُوَ رَبُّ ٱلْعَرْشِ ٱلْكَرِيمِ ﴿١١٦﴾ وَمَن يَدْعُ مَعَ ٱللَّهِ إِلَٰهًا
ءَاخَرَ لَا بُرْهَٰنَ لَهُۥ بِهِۦ فَإِنَّمَا حِسَابُهُۥ عِندَ رَبِّهِۦٓ ۚ إِنَّهُۥ لَا يُفْلِحُ
ٱلْكَٰفِرُونَ ﴿١١٧﴾ وَقُل رَّبِّ ٱغْفِرْ وَٱرْحَمْ وَأَنتَ خَيْرُ ٱلرَّٰحِمِينَ ﴿١١٨﴾

فَسُبْحَـٰنَ ٱللَّهِ حِينَ تُمْسُونَ
وَحِينَ تُصْبِحُونَ ﴿١٧﴾ وَلَهُ ٱلْحَمْدُ فِى ٱلسَّمَـٰوَٰتِ وَٱلْأَرْضِ
وَعَشِيًّا وَحِينَ تُظْهِرُونَ ﴿١٨﴾ يُخْرِجُ ٱلْحَىَّ مِنَ ٱلْمَيِّتِ وَيُخْرِجُ
ٱلْمَيِّتَ مِنَ ٱلْحَىِّ وَيُحْىِ ٱلْأَرْضَ بَعْدَ مَوْتِهَا ۚ
وَكَذَٰلِكَ تُخْرَجُونَ ﴿١٩﴾

أَعُوذُ بِاللّٰهِ السَّمِيعِ العَلِيمِ مِنَ الشَّيْطَانِ الرَّجِيمِ (ثلاثاً) *

لَوْ أَنزَلْنَا هَـٰذَا
ٱلْقُرْءَانَ عَلَىٰ جَبَلٍ لَّرَأَيْتَهُۥ خَـٰشِعًا مُّتَصَدِّعًا مِّنْ خَشْيَةِ
ٱللَّهِ ۚ وَتِلْكَ ٱلْأَمْثَـٰلُ نَضْرِبُهَا لِلنَّاسِ لَعَلَّهُمْ يَتَفَكَّرُونَ
﴿٢١﴾ هُوَ ٱللَّهُ ٱلَّذِى لَآ إِلَـٰهَ إِلَّا هُوَ ۖ عَـٰلِمُ ٱلْغَيْبِ وَٱلشَّهَـٰدَةِ ۖ
هُوَ ٱلرَّحْمَـٰنُ ٱلرَّحِيمُ ﴿٢٢﴾ هُوَ ٱللَّهُ ٱلَّذِى لَآ إِلَـٰهَ إِلَّا هُوَ
ٱلْمَلِكُ ٱلْقُدُّوسُ ٱلسَّلَـٰمُ ٱلْمُؤْمِنُ ٱلْمُهَيْمِنُ ٱلْعَزِيزُ
ٱلْجَبَّارُ ٱلْمُتَكَبِّرُ ۚ سُبْحَـٰنَ ٱللَّهِ عَمَّا يُشْرِكُونَ
﴿٢٣﴾ هُوَ ٱللَّهُ ٱلْخَـٰلِقُ ٱلْبَارِئُ ٱلْمُصَوِّرُ ۖ لَهُ ٱلْأَسْمَآءُ ٱلْحُسْنَىٰ ۚ
يُسَبِّحُ لَهُۥ مَا فِى ٱلسَّمَـٰوَٰتِ وَٱلْأَرْضِ ۖ وَهُوَ ٱلْعَزِيزُ ٱلْحَكِيمُ ﴿٢٤﴾

سَلَٰمٌ عَلَىٰ نُوحٍ فِي ٱلْعَٰلَمِينَ ﴿٧٩﴾ إِنَّا كَذَٰلِكَ نَجْزِي ٱلْمُحْسِنِينَ ﴿٨٠﴾
إِنَّهُۥ مِنْ عِبَادِنَا ٱلْمُؤْمِنِينَ ﴿٨١﴾

أَعُوذُ بِكَلِمَاتِ اللهِ التَّامَّاتِ مِن شَرِّ مَا خَلَقَ (ثلاثاً) * بِسمِ اللهِ الَّذِي لا يَضُرُّ مَعَ اسْمِهِ شَيءٌ فِي الأَرضِ ولا فِي السَّمَاءِ، وَهُوَ السَّمِيعُ العَلِيم (ثلاثاً) * اللَّهُمَّ إِنِّي أَصْبَحْتُ مِنْكَ فِي نِعْمَةٍ وَعَافِيَةٍ وَسِتْرٍ، فَأَتِمَّ نِعْمَتَكَ عَلَيَّ وَعَافِيَتَكَ وَسِتْرَكَ فِي الدُّنْيَا وَالآخِرَةِ (ثلاثاً) * اللَّهُمَّ إِنِّي أَصْبَحْتُ أُشْهِدُكَ، وَأُشْهِدُ حَمَلَةَ عَرْشِكَ، وَمَلائِكَتَكَ، وَجَمِيعَ خَلْقِكَ، أَنَّكَ أَنتَ اللهُ، لا إله إلا أَنتَ، وَحْدَكَ لا شَرِيكَ لَكَ، وَأَنَّ مُحَمَّداً عَبْدُكَ وَرَسُولُك (أربعاً) * الحَمْدُ لِلَّهِ رَبِّ العَالَمِين، حَمْداً يُوَافِي نِعَمَهُ وَيُكَافِئُ مَزِيدَه (ثلاثاً) * آمَنتُ بِاللهِ العَظِيم، وَكَفَرْتُ بِالجِبْتِ وَالطَّاغُوت، وَاسْتَمْسَكتُ بِالعُرْوَةِ الوُثقَى، لا انفِصَامَ لَهَا، وَاللهُ سَمِيعٌ عَلِيم (ثلاثاً) * رَضِيتُ بِاللهِ رَبّاً، وَبِالإسلامِ دِيناً، وَبِسَيِّدِنا مُحَمَّدٍ صَلَّى اللهُ عَلَيهِ وَسَلَّمَ، نَبِيّاً وَرَسُولا (ثلاثاً) *

حَسْبِيَ اللهُ لا إلهَ إلا هُوَ، عَلَيهِ تَوَكَّلْتُ، وَهُوَ رَبُّ العَرشِ العَظِيم (سبعاً) * اللّهُمَّ صَلِّ على سَيِّدِنَا مُحَمَّدٍ وَآلِهِ وَصَحْبِهِ وَسَلِّم (عَشراً) * اللّهُمَّ إنِّي أَسْأَلُكَ مِن فُجَاءَةِ الخَير، وَأَعُوذُ بِكَ مِن فُجَاءَةِ الشَّرّ * اللّهُمَّ أَنتَ رَبِّي، لا إله إلا أنت، خَلَقْتَني وَأَنَا عَبْدُك، وَأَنا على عَهْدِكَ وَوَعْدِكَ مَا اسْتَطَعْت، أَعُوذُ بِكَ مِن شَرِّ مَا صَنَعْت، أَبُوءُ لَكَ بِنِعْمَتِكَ عَلَيَّ وَأَبُوءُ بِذَنبِي، فَاغْفِرْلِي، فَإِنَّهُ لا يَغْفِرُ الذُّنُوبَ إلا أَنت * اللّهُمَّ أَنتَ رَبِّي لا إله إلا أَنت، عَلَيكَ تَوَكّلتُ، وَأَنتَ رَبُّ العَرشِ العَظِيم * مَاشَاءَ اللهُ كَان، وَمَا لَمْ يَشَأْ لَمْ يَكُن، وَلا حَوْلَ وَلا قُوَّةَ إلا بِاللّهِ العَلِيِّ العَظِيم * أَعْلَمُ أَنَّ اللهَ عَلى كُلِّ شَيءٍ قَدِير، وَأَنَّ اللهَ قَدْ أَحَاطَ بِكُلِّ شَيءٍ عِلْما * اللّهُمَّ إِنِّي أَعُوذُ بِكَ مِن شَرِّ نَفْسِي وَمِن شَرِّ كُلِّ دَابَّةٍ أَنتَ آخِذٌ بِنَاصِيَتِهَا، إنَّ رَبِّي عَلى صِرَاطٍ مُسْتَقِيم * يَاحَيُّ يَاقَيُّوم، بِرَحْمَتِكَ أَسْتَغِيثُ، وَمِن عَذَابِكَ أَسْتَجِير، أَصْلِحْ لِي شَأْنِي كُلَّهُ، وَلا تَكِلْنِي إلى نَفْسِي وَلا إلى أَحَدٍ مِن خَلْقِكَ طَرْفَةَ عَين *

اللّٰهُمَّ إنِّي أَعُوذُ بِكَ مِن الهَمِّ وَالحَزَن ، وَأَعُوذُ بِكَ مِن العَجْزِ وَالكَسَل ، وَأَعُوذُ بِكَ مِن الجُبْنِ وَالبُخْل ، وَأَعُوذُ بِكَ مِن غَلَبَةِ الدَّين وَقَهْرِ الرِّجَال * اللّٰهُمَّ إنِّي أَسْأَلُكَ العَفْوَ وَالعَافِيَةَ وَالمُعَافَاةَ الدَّائِمَةَ في دِينِي وَدُنيَايَ وَأَهْلِي وَمَالِي * اللّٰهُمَّ اسْتُرْ عَوْرَاتي وَآمِنْ رَوْعَاتي * اللّٰهُمَّ احْفَظْنِي مِن بَيْنِ يَدَيَّ وَمِن خَلْفِي ، وَعَنْ يَمِينِي وَعَنْ شِمَالِي وَمِن فَوْقِي ، وَأَعُوذُ بِعَظَمَتِكَ أَنْ أُغْتَالَ مِن تَحتِي * اللّٰهُمَّ أَنتَ خَلَقْتَنِي وَأَنتَ تَهْدِينِي ، وَأَنتَ تُطعِمُنِي وَأَنتَ تَسْقِينِي ، وَأَنتَ تُمِيتُنِي وَأَنتَ تُحْيِينِي * أَصْبَحْنَا عَلى فِطْرَةِ الإسْلام ، وَعَلى كَلِمَةِ الإخْلاص ، وَعَلى دِينِ نَبِيِّنَا مُحَمَّدٍ ، صَلَّى اللّٰهُ عَلَيهِ وَآلِهِ وَسَلَّم ، وَعَلى مِلَّةِ أَبِينَا إبْرَاهِيمَ ، حَنِيفاً ، مُسْلِماً ، وَمَا كَانَ مِنَ المُشْرِكِين * اللّٰهُمَّ بِكَ أَصْبَحْنَا ، وَبِكَ أَمْسَينَا ، وَبِكَ نَحْيَا ، وَبِكَ نَمُوتُ ، وَإلَيكَ النُّشُور * أَصْبَحْنَا وَأَصْبَحَ المُلْكُ لِلّٰه ، وَالحَمْدُ لِلّٰهِ رَبِّ العَالَمِين * اللّٰهُمَّ إنِّي أَسْأَلُكَ خيرَ هذَا اليَوم ، فَتْحَهُ ، وَنَصْرَهُ ، وَنُورَهُ ، وَبَرَكَتَهُ ، وَهُدَاه * اللّٰهُمَّ إنِّي أَسْأَلُكَ خَيْرَ هذَا اليَومِ وَخَيْرَ مَا فِيه ، وَأَعُوذُ بِكَ مِن

شَرِّ هذَا اليَومِ وَشَرِّ مَا فِيه * اللّهُمَّ مَا أَصْبَحَ بِي مِن نِعْمَةٍ أَو بِأَحَدٍ مِن خَلْقِكَ فَمِنْكَ وَحْدَكَ لا شَرِيكَ لَكَ ، فَلَكَ الحَمْدُ وَلَكَ الشُّكْرُ عَلى ذلِك * سُبْحَانَ اللهِ وَبِحَمْدِه (مائة مرَّة) * سُبْحَانَ اللهِ العَظِيم وَبِحَمْدِه (مائة مرَّة) * سُبْحَانَ اللهِ ، وَالحَمْدُ لِلّه ، وَلا إلهَ إلا اللهُ ، وَاللهُ أَكْبَر (مائة مرَّة) * وَيَزِيدُ صَبَاحاً : لا إلهَ إلا اللهُ وَحْدَهُ لا شَرِيكَ لَه ، لَهُ المُلْكُ وَلَهُ الحَمْد ، وَهُوَ عَلى كُلِّ شَيءٍ قَدِير (مائة مرَّة) *

وَيقُولُ فِي المَسَاءِ :

بَدَل أَصْبَحْت : أَمْسَيت

وَبَدَل النُشور : المَصِير

ARABIC APPENDIX II: *Al-Rātib al-Shahīr*

الرَّاتِب الشَّهِير

بِسْمِ ٱللَّهِ ٱلرَّحْمَٰنِ ٱلرَّحِيمِ ﴿١﴾
ٱلْحَمْدُ لِلَّهِ رَبِّ ٱلْعَٰلَمِينَ ﴿٢﴾ ٱلرَّحْمَٰنِ ٱلرَّحِيمِ ﴿٣﴾
مَٰلِكِ يَوْمِ ٱلدِّينِ ﴿٤﴾ إِيَّاكَ نَعْبُدُ وَإِيَّاكَ
نَسْتَعِينُ ﴿٥﴾ ٱهْدِنَا ٱلصِّرَٰطَ ٱلْمُسْتَقِيمَ ﴿٦﴾
صِرَٰطَ ٱلَّذِينَ أَنْعَمْتَ عَلَيْهِمْ غَيْرِ ٱلْمَغْضُوبِ
عَلَيْهِمْ وَلَا ٱلضَّآلِّينَ ﴿٧﴾

ٱللَّهُ لَآ إِلَٰهَ إِلَّا هُوَۖ
ٱلۡحَيُّ ٱلۡقَيُّومُۚ لَا تَأۡخُذُهُۥ سِنَةٞ وَلَا نَوۡمٞۚ لَّهُۥ مَا فِي ٱلسَّمَٰوَٰتِ وَمَا
فِي ٱلۡأَرۡضِۗ مَن ذَا ٱلَّذِي يَشۡفَعُ عِندَهُۥٓ إِلَّا بِإِذۡنِهِۦۚ يَعۡلَمُ مَا بَيۡنَ
أَيۡدِيهِمۡ وَمَا خَلۡفَهُمۡۖ وَلَا يُحِيطُونَ بِشَيۡءٖ مِّنۡ عِلۡمِهِۦٓ إِلَّا بِمَا
شَآءَۚ وَسِعَ كُرۡسِيُّهُ ٱلسَّمَٰوَٰتِ وَٱلۡأَرۡضَۖ وَلَا يَـُٔودُهُۥ حِفۡظُهُمَاۚ
وَهُوَ ٱلۡعَلِيُّ ٱلۡعَظِيمُ ﴿٢٥٥﴾

ءَامَنَ ٱلرَّسُولُ بِمَآ أُنزِلَ
إِلَيۡهِ مِن رَّبِّهِۦ وَٱلۡمُؤۡمِنُونَۚ كُلٌّ ءَامَنَ بِٱللَّهِ وَمَلَٰٓئِكَتِهِۦ وَكُتُبِهِۦ
وَرُسُلِهِۦ لَا نُفَرِّقُ بَيۡنَ أَحَدٖ مِّن رُّسُلِهِۦۚ وَقَالُواْ سَمِعۡنَا
وَأَطَعۡنَاۖ غُفۡرَانَكَ رَبَّنَا وَإِلَيۡكَ ٱلۡمَصِيرُ ﴿٢٨٥﴾ لَا يُكَلِّفُ
ٱللَّهُ نَفۡسًا إِلَّا وُسۡعَهَاۚ لَهَا مَا كَسَبَتۡ وَعَلَيۡهَا مَا ٱكۡتَسَبَتۡۗ
رَبَّنَا لَا تُؤَاخِذۡنَآ إِن نَّسِينَآ أَوۡ أَخۡطَأۡنَاۚ رَبَّنَا وَلَا تَحۡمِلۡ
عَلَيۡنَآ إِصۡرٗا كَمَا حَمَلۡتَهُۥ عَلَى ٱلَّذِينَ مِن قَبۡلِنَاۚ رَبَّنَا وَلَا
تُحَمِّلۡنَا مَا لَا طَاقَةَ لَنَا بِهِۦۖ وَٱعۡفُ عَنَّا وَٱغۡفِرۡ لَنَا وَٱرۡحَمۡنَآۚ
أَنتَ مَوۡلَىٰنَا فَٱنصُرۡنَا عَلَى ٱلۡقَوۡمِ ٱلۡكَٰفِرِينَ ﴿٢٨٦﴾

لا إلهَ إلا اللّٰهُ وَحْدَهُ لا شَرِيكَ لَه ، لَهُ المُلْكُ وَلَهُ الحَمْدُ ، يُحْيِي وَيُمِيتُ وَهُوَ عَلى كُلِّ شَيءٍ قَدِير (ثلاثاً) * سُبْحَانَ اللّٰهِ ، وَالحَمْدُ لِلّٰهِ ، وَلا إلهَ إلا اللّٰهُ ، وَاللّٰهُ أَكْبَر (ثلاثاً) * سُبْحَانَ اللّٰهِ وَبِحَمْدِهِ ، سُبْحَانَ اللّٰهِ العَظِيم (ثلاثاً) * رَبَّنَا اغْفِرْ لَنَا وَتُبْ عَلَينا ، إِنَّكَ أَنتَ التَّوَّابُ الرَّحِيم (ثلاثاً) * اللّٰهُمَّ صَلِّ عَلى مُحَمَّدٍ ، اللّٰهُمَّ صَلِّ عَلَيهِ وَسَلِّم (ثلاثاً) * أَعُوذُ بِكَلِمَاتِ اللّٰهِ التَّامَّاتِ مِن شَرِّ مَا خَلَق (ثلاثاً) * بِسْمِ اللّٰهِ الَّذِي لا يَضُرُّ مَعَ اسْمِهِ شَيءٌ فِي الأَرْضِ وَلا فِي السَّمَاءِ ، وَهُوَ السَّمِيعُ العَلِيم (ثلاثاً) * رَضِينَا بِاللّٰهِ رَبّاً ، وَبِالإِسْلام دِيناً ، وَبِمُحَمَّدٍ نَبِيّا (ثلاثاً) * بِسْمِ اللّٰهِ ، وَالحَمْدُ لِلّٰه ، وَالخَيرُ وَالشَّرُّ بِمَشِيئَةِ اللّٰه (ثلاثاً) * آمَنَّا بِاللّٰهِ وَاليَوْمِ الآخِرْ ، تُبْنَا إلى اللّٰهِ بَاطِناً وَظَاهِرْ (ثلاثاً) * يَا رَبَّنَا وَاعْفُ عَنَّا ، وَامْحُ الَّذِي كَانَ مِنَّا (ثلاثاً) * يَاذَا الجَلالِ وَالإِكْرام ، أَمِتْنَا عَلى دِينِ الإِسْلام (سبعاً) * يَاقَوِيُّ يَامَتِين ، اِكْفِ شَرَّ الظَّالِمِين (ثلاثاً) * أَصْلَحَ اللّٰهُ أُمُورَ المُسْلِمِين ، صَرَفَ اللّٰهُ شَرَّ المُؤْذِين (ثلاثاً) *

يَاعَلِيُّ يَاكَبِير ، يَاعَلِيمُ يَاقَدِير ، يَاسَمِيعُ يَابَصِير ، يَالَطِيفُ يَاخَبِير (ثلاثاً) * يَافَارِجَ الهَمّ ، يَاكَاشِفَ الغَمّ ، يَامَن لِعَبْدِهِ يَغْفِرُ وَيَرْحَم (ثلاثاً) * أَسْتَغْفِرُ اللّٰهَ رَبَّ البَرَايَا ، أَسْتَغْفِرُ اللّٰهَ مِنَ الخَطَايَا (أربعاً) * لا إلهَ إلا اللّٰهُ (خمسين مرّةً وإن بلّغها إلى ألفٍ كان حسَناً) * مُحَمَّدٌ رَسُولُ اللّٰهِ ، صَلَّى اللّٰهُ عَلَيهِ وَآلِهِ وَسَلَّمَ ، وَشَرَّفَ وَكَرَّمَ ، وَمَجَّدَ وَعَظَّمَ ، وَرَضِيَ اللّٰهُ عَن أَهْلِ بَيْتِهِ الطَّيِّبِينَ الطَّاهِرِين ، وَأَصْحَابِهِ الأَخْيَارِ المُهْتَدِين ، وَالتَّابِعِينَ لَهُمْ بِإِحْسَانٍ إلى يَومِ الدِّين *

بِسْمِ ٱللَّهِ ٱلرَّحْمَٰنِ ٱلرَّحِيمِ

قُلْ هُوَ ٱللَّهُ أَحَدٌ ﴿١﴾ ٱللَّهُ ٱلصَّمَدُ ﴿٢﴾ لَمْ يَلِدْ وَلَمْ يُولَدْ ﴿٣﴾ وَلَمْ يَكُن لَّهُۥ كُفُوًا أَحَدٌۢ ﴿٤﴾ (ثلاثاً)

بِسْمِ ٱللَّهِ ٱلرَّحْمَٰنِ ٱلرَّحِيمِ

قُلْ أَعُوذُ بِرَبِّ ٱلْفَلَقِ ﴿١﴾ مِن شَرِّ مَا خَلَقَ ﴿٢﴾ وَمِن شَرِّ غَاسِقٍ إِذَا وَقَبَ ﴿٣﴾ وَمِن شَرِّ ٱلنَّفَّٰثَٰتِ فِى ٱلْعُقَدِ ﴿٤﴾ وَمِن شَرِّ حَاسِدٍ إِذَا حَسَدَ ﴿٥﴾

بِسْمِ ٱللَّهِ ٱلرَّحْمَٰنِ ٱلرَّحِيمِ

قُلْ أَعُوذُ بِرَبِّ ٱلنَّاسِ ﴿١﴾ مَلِكِ ٱلنَّاسِ ﴿٢﴾ إِلَٰهِ
ٱلنَّاسِ ﴿٣﴾ مِن شَرِّ ٱلْوَسْوَاسِ ٱلْخَنَّاسِ ﴿٤﴾ ٱلَّذِى
يُوَسْوِسُ فِى صُدُورِ ٱلنَّاسِ ﴿٥﴾
مِنَ ٱلْجِنَّةِ وَٱلنَّاسِ ﴿٦﴾

الفاتِحَةُ إلى كَافَّةِ عِبادِ اللهِ الصّالِحين، وَلِوالِدَينا ، وَجَميعِ المؤْمِنِينَ وَالمُؤمِنَاتِ وَالمُسْلِمِينَ وَالمُسْلِمات ، أَنَّ اللهَ يَغْفِرُ لَهُم وَيَرحَمُهُم ، وَيَنفَعُنا بِأَسْرارِهِم وَبَرَكَاتِهِم . . . وَإِلى حَضْرَةِ النَّبِيِّ مُحَمَّدٍ صَلَّى اللهُ عَلَيهِ وَسَلَّم *

اللّهُمَّ إِنّا نَسْأَلُكَ رِضَاكَ وَالجَنَّة ، وَنَعُوذُ بِكَ مِن سَخَطِكَ وَالنّار *